Paint Smart, not Hard

All the tips, tricks, and strategies you need to use to start a profitable house painting business immediately.

By Jeff Lockwood

Publisher – Painting Biz Publishing

Cover Photography and Graphics by Jeff Lockwood

ISBN: 9798332668743

Copyright 2024, All rights reserved.

No part of this book may be produced, transmitted, or distributed in any form or by any means, electronic, mechanical, photocopying, recorded, scanning or otherwise without permission from the author.

This book is designed to provide accurate information and authoritative information regarding the subject matter covered. This information is given with the understanding that neither the author nor its agents, employees, vendors, or assigns guarantees your outcomes using the information contained in this book.

Table of Contents

Disclaimer/Terms of Use Agreement — 4

About the Author — 5

Symbol and their Meanings — 6

Dedication — 7

Acknowledgements — 9

Author's Introduction — 14

Chapter 1 – My Best Advice for You
Here's the best advice that I can give to you. — 21

Chapter 2 - What Equipment & Tools You Need
What tools and equipment will you need and why. — 43

Chapter 3 – All About Buying Paint. — 53
Whom to buy paint from and why you should.

Chapter 4 - Marketing Strategies Advice — 56
What marketing has worked for me and what hasn't.

Chapter 5 – Local Networking Opportunities — 78
Which ones are worth the time and investment?

Chapter 6 – Estimating Jobs So You Make Money — 81
The best, the fastest way and it makes you profit.

Chapter 7 – I Need Painting Help — 88
Where to find painters when you need help.

Chapter 8 – My Final Thoughts   100
    Just a little bit of encouragement going forward.

Chapter 9 - My List of Painting Business Books   101
    You should read my list of favorite painting business books.

Appendix A - How to make a Hanging Bucket   104
    A guide to making your own Paint Brush Hanging Bucket. Helps make cleaning brushes easier.

Appendix B - Anatomy of a Paint Brush   105
    It's important for a pro painter to know how a paint actually brush works.

Appendix C – Pro Painter Quiz and Answers   110
    A pro painter test that I use when hiring new painters.

Appendix D – Average Painting Square Footage Hours   122
    Great info for estimating interior painting projects.

Appendix E – Names of Various Parts of a House   123
    Knowing the names of house parts is important.

Disclaimer/Terms of Use Agreement

There is no guarantee of success and/or that you will make money, either written or implied. The author/publisher specifically disclaims any personal liability, loss, risk incurred because of acting on, undertaking, or relaying any advice or information presented herein.

While all attempts have been made to verify information provided in this book, neither the author nor the publisher assumes any responsibility for errors or omissions or contradictory interpretation of the subject matter herein.

This book is not intended to be used as a source of legal or business advice. Please remember that the information contained may be subject to varying state, provincial or local laws or regulations that may apply to the user's particular practice.

The purchaser or reader of this book assumes responsibility for the use of these materials and information. Adherence to all applicable laws and regulations, both federal, state, provincial and local governing professional licensing, business practices, advertising, and any other aspects of doing business in the USA or Canada or any other jurisdiction is the sole responsibility of the purchaser or reader.

About the Author

Jeff Lockwood is the author of the Amazon best-selling book *Pro Painter Q & A.* With over 15 years of experience as a successful painting contractor, Jeff has always been passionate about helping struggling painters get their businesses on the right track. He provides expert advice on equipment, sales, marketing, business networking, proper estimating, and production systems—all with the goal of helping painters achieve financial stability and enjoy more personal freedom, allowing for more time with family and friends.

Since 2008, Jeff has been operating his own painting company in South-Western Ontario, Canada, during which time his company has won numerous local Reader's Choice Business Awards. His company is a proud member of the Grey Bruce Home Builders & Trades Association (OHBA/CHBA), the Thornbury Home Builders & Trades Association, and the Painting Contractors Association (**www.pcapainted.org**).

In 2024, Jeff was invited to speak on the expert panel "How to Become a Selling Machine" at the Painting Contractors Association Expo at Disney World in Orlando, Florida.

Jeff lives in Chatsworth, Ontario, with his wife Valerie and enjoys spending time with his three wonderful grandchildren. He also offers nationwide painting business coaching through his website, **paintingbizcoach.com**.

To contact Jeff for mentoring, coaching, or speaking at your painting-related event, email him at **jeff@paintingbizcoach.com**.

Symbols and their Meanings

Throughout this book you will occasionally see various symbols beside paragraphs. These are indicators for various things like book recommendations, helpful business tips, etc.

 When you see the "paint brush" symbol it's just a symbol to separate chapters in the book.

 The "book" symbol it's a sign that I am giving a quick review of a painting business related book that I would recommend that you should buy and read.

 The "magic hat" symbol it's a sign that I am giving a helpful painting trick or a magic painting business tip.

 The "story page" symbol, it's a sign that I am sharing a story about something specific that I think will be helpful to you if you have something similar happen to you.

 The "fun fact lightbulb "symbol, it's a sign that I am sharing a fun and interesting painting business fact with you.

Dedication

This book is dedicated to the people who mean the most to me in the world—my family. To my wife, Valerie, who works beside me every day in our family painting business. Without her hard work, unwavering support, and constant encouragement, I would not have achieved as much as I have. Thank you for always standing by my side and reminding me during the stressful times that "everything will be alright."

A family work photo of Valerie, Jeff, Myles, Onna and Lucas. The photo was taken by Nicole Mills in 2019.

To my wonderful family, who continue to work with me—or have worked with me—over the years in the painting business, all except for Bryon, despite my best efforts to hire him. Yes, my son-in-law Bryon is a talented and successful professional painter in his own right, completely independent of me.

Fortunately, he grew up in his family's painting business, learning from his father, Paul. Conversations with Bryon always make for lively discussions around the dinner table, often revolving around the painting industry—one of my favorite topics. I truly appreciate all the support my family has given me.

It has helped turn ideas like this book into reality.
Thank you to each of you for everything you do for Valerie, me, and our small family business.

Our newest family work photo was taken in 2024. From left to right – Lucas, Nash, Jeff, Myles, Valerie and Onna. Photo was taken by Carly Martin.

Acknowledgements

To my friends, Brenda and Martin: Without the business knowledge and experience I gained from working alongside both of you and your family for over a decade, I might have given up on the brush right from the start. The stories your mother shared with me about the early days of your family business prepared me for the challenges I would face with mine. Like your parents, I persevered through the business hurdles and financial hardships that came in those early years. Your support and example were invaluable to me.

To Diane, who gave me my first opportunity as a professional painter, and to the brothers, Jeff and Chris, who taught me the processes of new residential construction painting: The guidance you offered at the beginning of my painting career has always meant so much. It laid the foundation for building my own successful painting business.

To Roland, who passed away during the writing of this book. When I first started out on my own, Roland worked with me part-time, offering his support in those early days.

Here's a photo of Roland painting in a small space. I took it during the years we painted together. There was never a dull moment with Roland around, he was always doing something crazy or had an interesting painting story to tell me. Photo was taken by Jeff Lockwood.

Roland was my "go-to" guy whenever I needed help. Many of the painting tips and tricks he taught me are still used by my painting crew today. Thank you, Roland, for sharing all the knowledge you gained over your decades of professional painting. It will always be deeply appreciated. Rest in peace, my friend.

To one of my best friends, Kevin: Having been involved in his brother Allan's renovation business all his life, Kevin always had plenty of useful tips and tricks to share with me. Two pieces of advice, in particular, have always stuck with me.

Every year, without fail, Kevin would work with me for a couple of weeks. When I first started painting professionally, one of the first things he noticed was that I had been taught to paint a room the wrong way. He said, "It's best to cut in one wall at a time and then immediately roll that wall. Don't cut in the whole room and then roll it all at once, you'll just end up standing around watching paint dry. That has always proven to be great advice.

Kevin also taught me something invaluable about pricing. He said to me – "always charge what you're worth." I used to feel bad charging what seemed like a lot of money for a painting project, often wanting to give customers a "good deal." Kevin would say, "Do you own a million-dollar cottage?" I'd reply, "No, I don't." And he'd remind me, "Then don't feel bad. Always charge what you're worth." More great advice that I continue to live by. Thank you for that, Kevin.

Lockwood Painting staff group photo of 2019 staff – Joe, Nicole, Doug, Donna-Lea, Jeff, Valerie, Shawn, Lucas, Onna and Myles. Photo taken by Nicole Mills.

Lockwood Painting 2020 staff – Mike, Paul, Myles, Onna, Lucas, Pat, Nicole, Donna-Lea, (front) Jeff and Valerie. Photos taken by Nicole Mills.

A Lockwood Painting staff group photo of my 2024 painting crew. Jay, Scott, Donna-Lea, Travis, Lucas, Valerie, Jeff, Myles, Onna, Nash, Joe, Curtis, Carter and Tammy. Photo was taken by Carly Martin.

To all the painters and subcontractors who have worked with me over the years, thank you for your hard work and dedication—not just to my company, but to the residential painting industry as a whole.

While I may not remember the names of every painter that has worked for me, there are a few that stand out over the years and aren't already mentioned in the photos included in this book: Rusty (rest in peace), Brad, Travis, Todd, Taylor, Shawn (rest in peace), Ron, Ryan, Lisa, Sarah, Rob, Bryden, Ken, Jeremy, and so many others. Thanks for all the memories.

I also want to extend my gratitude to the paint sales representatives who have supported me throughout the years: Michael Ragot from Benjamin Moore, and Steve Hardy, Mark Zebedee, and Lucas Loder from Sherwin-Williams. Your help and guidance have always been greatly appreciated.

Finally, to Donna-Lea, my friend, business colleague, and trusted assistant: Without your dedication, hard work, and the wealth of knowledge and skills you've brought from the decorating industry into the painting business I started nearly two decades ago, I would never have had the time to write this book. Our collaboration over the past eight years has been instrumental in growing the company. Thank you for all you have done in the past and for everything you continue to do.

Author's Introduction

There's nothing quite like starting your own business to make you feel financially independent and free. Ever since I was a child, I knew deep down that I wanted to be a business owner someday. Little did I realize it would take me until the age of 37 to find the right business that truly worked for me. Over my 50-plus years on this planet, I've started several different businesses.

 ***If you are just starting out in your own painting business, Arthur Cole's book "The Business of Painting" is worth reading. His book has a good, solid foundation of information for the painting contractor that really wants to start his or her business out on the right track. Yes, it's available on Amazon.***

The first business I ever started was a window cleaning company called "Squeaky Clean Window Services," inspired by a similar business my cousin Bobby Lockwood had started in Hamilton, Ontario. I was 19 years old at the time. I landed two commercial contracts—one cleaning atrium windows at a local fast-food restaurant and another cleaning storefront windows for a pizza shop across town.

I also cleaned residential windows here and there. It was more of a side hustle, as I still had a full-time job working as a Swing Manager at the local McDonald's. All of that was just enough to keep me busy—and out of trouble.

The second business I started a few years later was a graphic design and digital printing business.

I designed and printed business cards, letterheads, and flyers for about a dozen small business clients. I also created, printed, and sold advertising spots on table placemats that were distributed by several local restaurants. However, like my previous venture, it ended up being more of a side hustle.

About a decade later, I started another small side business offering bartending services for weddings and special events, mostly during the summer months. While it sometimes felt like a lot of extra work for little profit, it was a great way to earn some vacation money.

I was almost 40 when I finally started my painting company. After 13 years of working at a family-owned furniture manufacturing business, I lost my job. Around the same time, my first wife and I separated, so I found myself not only without a job, but without my wife, my dog, and my house.

Suddenly, money became a serious concern, and I needed to come up with a new career path quickly. Prior to working at the furniture factory, I had held various sales positions. I had worked in sales for a small printing company, handled sales and merchandising for a national beverage company, and worked in sales for a local cable television company that also offered digital printing, internet, and multimedia services. That company had cutting-edge technology for the time—we were the first in the area to introduce direct-to-copier digital printing and establish a locally-based internet service.

Overall, none of those earlier business ventures amounted to much, but the painting company turned out to be something entirely different. My uncle Lou, a very successful businessman before his retirement, once told me, "Concentrate on just one thing. Know everything about it, and you will be successful." At the time, we were discussing stock market investments, but I realized that advice could just as easily apply to my business.

So, we gave up the bartending and catering side hustle and focused entirely on the painting company, without any distractions. I threw myself into learning everything I could about house painting, reading and absorbing all the knowledge I could find.

Business Tip – When your local paint store hosts a product or equipment demonstration, make it a priority to attend. You'd be surprised at how much you can learn. Plus, the networking opportunities with other local painters are invaluable.

I've always been drawn to house painting for one reason or another, and I'm pretty sure it had something to do with the potential earnings I'd heard about. Although I had never done any professional painting before, I decided to focus on it as my new career and dive into the painting and decorating trade, with the hope of starting my own business someday.

Did you know that a residential painting business is one of the few types of businesses that can thrive in almost any economic situation? People and businesses always need painting services. During the Great Depression (1929–1939), for example, people stayed in their homes rather than selling, and many chose to fix them up—painting was a big part of that.

Similarly, during the COVID-19 pandemic (2019–2021), the demand for painting services surged. With everyone stuck at home, people were eager to make improvements, and since painting contractors were still allowed to work, we found ourselves busier than ever.

Painting is one of the most inexpensive ways that people can fix up their homes. Most homeowners tell me that they would rather hire a painter to paint than to try and do it themselves.

Residential house painting really is a recession proof business. It's also a great business to be in when the economy is thriving, and people are selling their homes. One of the first things a real estate agent advises clients to do is give their home a fresh coat of paint to help close the sale.

But I had one obstacle: I needed someone to teach me how to paint professionally. Other than spraying a clear coat on furniture during my time at the factory, I had no real painting experience. So, I decided to put up a post on a local internet classified site where many painters in my area advertised their services. I posted that I was looking for a painting company willing to take me on as an inexperienced apprentice.

That idea worked like a charm. Within a few days, I received a call from a local residential painting company owned by a woman named Diane. After a quick interview, I was hired and started working with her and her two-person crew. We primarily did small interior repaints with the occasional exterior project. As a beginner, I learned the basics of painting—how to set up, clean up, and prep a room before painting. I was taught how to cut in with a 2.5-inch brush and roll with a 9-inch roller—the very fundamentals.

Fun Fact – Did you know that the size of a roller sleeve sold in the United States and a roller sleeve sold in Canada are different sizes? In the US a standard roller sleeve is 9 inches long. In Canada they are 9 ½ inches long.

This went on for about six months, and it was a great experience. I discovered that I genuinely enjoyed house painting. There was something deeply satisfying about learning a skill and then using it to create something that pleased others. I loved the sense of accomplishment at the end of each job, knowing I had completed something worthwhile.

After leaving Diane's company, I was hired by another local painting business. The owner, Jeff, and his brother, Chris, were third-generation painters, both incredibly knowledgeable and skilled in the trade.

During my time working with them, they generously shared their vast painting expertise, especially in new home construction painting. However, winter arrived a few months later, and like many painters in the snow belt of Southwestern Ontario, I was laid off due to the seasonal slowdown in work.

 *An Industry Niche – Did you know that a 2022 survey found that 57% of painting companies work primarily with residential clients? This is something to consider when you're developing your business plan.*

So, I decided—perhaps a bit too hastily—to venture out on my own and start my own painting company. Yes, this had always been my plan.

However, in hindsight, I now realize I should have stayed with a company for a couple more years to fully learn the painting trade. But, as they say, the rest is history. Over the next decade, I would spend countless hours learning the trade the hard way. What I didn't anticipate were the many business challenges that would hit me right at the start of my new career.

It was tough not knowing how to find enough work to keep myself painting full time. Through trial and error (and plenty of mistakes), I eventually figured it out. Understanding proper pricing, effective marketing, and successful lead generation are essential skills you really need to master before venturing out on your own.

By sharing my experiences in this book, I hope to help you avoid the costly mistakes I made when starting out. I also hope the advice within will help you achieve profitability much faster than it took me.

If you're new to the painting trade or just beginning your own painting business, here are a few words of encouragement:

"No one is born with the ability to paint like a master painter. It takes time, practice and patience to improve your painting skills. It's very crucial to remember that everyone progresses with painting at a different pace."

During my time with the first painting company I worked for, my boss pulled me aside early one morning. She told me that after watching me over the past six weeks, she didn't think I was going to make it as a professional painter. She said my skills weren't developing as quickly as they should. However, she also mentioned that I was a hard worker and wanted to keep me on as an employee—just not as a painter.

Fast forward 16 years, and here I am, with the help of a strong lead-hand, running a successful painting company that generates nearly a million dollars a year. As for my first boss? She found the painting business too challenging and shut down her company after about five years.

So, here are my words of encouragement: Have faith in yourself. Learn everything you can about the painting trade and the business side of it. Understand how to price jobs correctly, ensuring that your company makes a profit, not just a wage for yourself. Don't be distracted by what other local painters are doing or saying. Set your own goals and push forward to succeed.

At the end of this book, I've included several resources that I've found useful over the years. These are located in the "Appendices" section. You'll find instructions on how to build a brush hanger bucket, a tool I've found handy for speeding up the brush cleaning process. There's also a section called "Anatomy of a Paint Brush," which I found interesting as it explains how our most-used tool is created and functions.

Additionally, there's an appendix featuring a list of "Average Painting Square Footage Hours," which provides a rough idea of how long it takes to paint different parts of a room—ceilings, walls, trim, baseboards, and doors—based on square footage. This has been extremely helpful when estimating jobs.

Finally, I've included diagrams of the "Various Parts of a House" to familiarize yourself with the terms for both interior and exterior elements that we often paint. Knowing these terms will help you when estimating and invoicing.

I hope you find these resources helpful. Good luck, and I wish you the best of success in the painting trade. Thank you to everyone who has taken the time to read my book—your support is very much appreciated.

- Notes -

Chapter 1 – The Best Advice I Can Give

When starting out on your own, begin small and gradually work your way up.

The best advice I can give to anyone thinking about starting their own painting company, or improving the one they've already begun, is contained in this chapter. If you're only going to read one chapter of this book, make it this one. Why? Because it offers the most critical information when it comes to operating a successful residential painting business.

I recently came across a harsh but resonant quote on Facebook that reflects the current state of the painting industry and the lack of business education available to painters. It said, *"Most painting contractors have no business being in business,"* and attributed this to *"the painting business owner's lack of understanding of the business side of painting."*

Two things from this post stood out to me, which is why I've included it here. First, I agree that *"most painting contractors have no business being in business."* This is absolutely true. Just because you know how to use a paintbrush doesn't mean you have what it takes to start and run a profitable painting company. Over the years, I've seen many residential painting businesses start up and quickly shut down—most of them not lasting more than a couple of years.

Why? In my opinion, it's because they lack a fundamental understanding of how to run a business. They don't have the business background or knowledge to manage a company profitably.

Moreover, many lack the drive necessary to sustain a business. They don't know the current labor rates in their area or how to accurately price jobs. After covering their expenses, they often realize they're not making any money, but it typically takes a year or so before they figure it out—and by then, they're ready to give up and leave the painting industry altogether.

Business Tip – Painter's rates can vary significantly from state to state and province to province. Asking someone in Atlanta, Georgia what they charge to paint a bedroom won't be helpful if you're working out of Las Vegas, Nevada. It's crucial to research the rates that are standard in your specific geographic area.

I know it may seem like starting a painting company is a simple task. You buy a ladder, a couple of drop sheets, some brushes, roller sleeves, roller cages, print a few business cards, and you're good to go, right? While it might look that easy, starting and running a **profitable** painting company can be quite challenging. I highlighted the word "profitable" for a reason. I often hear what new painters are charging for their services, and when I do the math, I realize some of them are working for less than minimum wage after expenses. I can't help but think they'd be better off stocking shelves at the local grocery store, which probably pays more with far less stress.

My best advice is to start your painting company slowly. Start small and scale up gradually. Begin by painting as a side hustle for friends, co-workers, relatives, and neighbors. Build a reputation, gather references, and establish yourself in the community.

More importantly, make sure you have another source of income to support you during the early stages of your business.

Make sure you have a steady source of income during your startup phase—something outside of your painting company.

When I started my painting company, I went all in right away. The best advice I can give is this: **Don't do that.** It didn't always work out well for me, and it likely won't for you either. Cash flow quickly becomes a major issue.

For the first few years, I constantly struggled and worried about having enough cash on hand. Sound familiar to anyone.

 **Here's a personal story:** It was January, and I had just been laid off from the painting company I had been working for. I figured I had nothing left to lose, so I decided to go out on my own and start my own painting company.

And with that, my painting company was born. Now what? The problem was, the country was in the middle of a recession, and I had no work lined up before starting my business. I didn't have a marketing plan in place to help me find jobs, and there was no money coming in. I needed funds to buy extra equipment—maybe even a paint sprayer. Since I had just been laid off from the painting company I worked for, I thought I'd apply for government unemployment benefits.

During the online application, I was asked if I had started my own business since the last time I was on unemployment. Proudly, I answered, "Yes." That proud answer, however, automatically disqualified me from receiving unemployment benefits. Are you kidding me? Yet another potential source of income—gone.

If you're in a similar situation, it's important to find a job that won't interfere with a typical 9-to-5, Monday-to-Friday painting schedule. Consider working in the evenings at places like Subway, McDonald's, or, even better, making deliveries for a local pizza shop.

At least while making deliveries in upscale neighborhoods, you can drop off a few door hangers for your painting company. By working part-time in the evenings, you'll still have time to paint during the day or on weekends.

Once you develop a steady stream of jobs, you'll be able to give up the part-time gig and paint full-time. For me, it took over a year before I began to see a consistent flow of jobs. As I mentioned earlier, those early days were tough financially.

Ensure you have a source of financing available in case you need immediate access to funds.

In his book *Paint Contractor's Business Manual* (available on Amazon), painter and author Kevin McGreer points out that one of the primary reasons painting businesses fail is due to cash flow problems.

You'll need a reliable source of financing—somewhere you can borrow money quickly when needed. Whether it's to support you during slow periods, cover delayed payments from clients, purchase necessary equipment, or pay for regular expenses when your bank account is low, having access to funds is crucial.

I'd recommend having at least $30,000 to $50,000 in available credit at any given time. Consider speaking with your bank about obtaining a personal line of credit. When I started my painting company, I took a page from Hollywood screenwriter and actor Kevin Smith's playbook. When he needed $30,000 to finance his first movie (*Clerks*), he applied for and used multiple credit cards while working as a video store manager. I thought this was a brilliant idea, so I did something similar for my painting business.

Thanks to my previous career in the furniture manufacturing industry, I had an excellent credit score.

At the time, I had one personal credit card with a $30,000 limit, and I decided to use it to finance my entire painting business.

That card allowed me to secure high credit limits at local paint stores, cover fuel costs for my truck to get to and from job sites and fund my early advertising campaigns in the local newspaper. I even used it to pay my subcontractor painters when needed.

 **Fun Fact – Did you know that the average estimate-to-job ratio for a contractor in the United States is 3 to 1? In other words, for every three estimates you give, you should be landing one job. If you're not, it's time to make some changes.**

I relied heavily on that card during my first few years as a self-employed house painter just to get by. Without it, I'm not sure how I would have made it through those slow and lean early years. The key takeaway here is to ensure you have access to some form of financing—because at some point, you will need it.

Start your company's marketing plan immediately. Without marketing, you won't secure a steady stream of work.

Getting painting jobs through word of mouth is great, especially since it's usually free, but from experience, I can tell you not to rely solely on that. Make sure you have a solid marketing plan in place and start some form of consistent advertising for your company right away.

To keep yourself—just one painter—busy with good-paying jobs, you should plan to spend around $250 per month on marketing. As you bring more painters on board, be sure to increase your advertising budget, accordingly, allocating additional funds for each painter.

Whether it's Google ads, Facebook ads, direct mailers, or door hangers, you'll need to invest that minimum amount to maintain a steady stream of work—what I really mean is "estimate opportunities"—for you and everyone working with you.

Make sure you know how to accurately and effectively price a job. Proper pricing is crucial for maintaining profitability while staying competitive. It's important to factor in all costs, including labor, materials, overhead, and a reasonable profit margin. Underpricing can leave you working for less than you're worth, while overpricing could cost you potential clients. Take the time to learn your local market rates, understand your expenses, and ensure your estimates are both fair and sustainable.

One of the biggest mistakes people make when starting a painting business is incorrect estimating. It's essential to know how to price jobs efficiently for your specific location. If you're fortunate, your boss at the successful painting company you currently work for may be willing to teach you how to estimate and price jobs.

If not, consider finding a painting mentor or business coach who can guide you through the process. Remember, residential painting rates vary significantly from city to city, state to state, and even country to country, so it's crucial to tailor your pricing to your local market.

 **An Industry Niche –** Did you know that a recent PCA survey of professional painters revealed that 57% of respondents identified as residential only painters, 23% as both residential and commercial painters, 11% as commercial-only painters, 6% as industrial-only painters, and 3% as specializing in other areas.

What a professional painter can charge in New York City is likely very different from what a painter just outside of Bowling Green, Kentucky, can charge. Investigating and understanding the rates that work for your geographical area is a crucial key to running a successful painting business—but it's not the only key. Knowing your local rates can mean the difference between painting smart and painting very hard for your money.

Need help with estimating? I cover developing relevant rates in Chapter 6, but additional estimating resources are available through the Painting Contractors Association. They offer a detailed guidebook on painting costs and estimating, which you can find on their website at www.pcapainted.org.

Author Dennis Gleason also publishes a book called the *National Painting Cost Estimator*, with updated rates released annually. You can find the latest version for purchase on Amazon. There are several online business tools that can help with estimating painting projects.

Here are a few you can explore:

Paint Scout is an estimating software specifically designed for painting contractors. It helps streamline the process of creating accurate and professional estimates based on labor, materials, and job specifics. With features that allow for detailed cost breakdowns and job tracking, PaintScout enables contractors to price jobs correctly and manage projects more efficiently, ultimately boosting profitability and improving workflow. For more information, you can visit their website at **www.paintscout.com**.

DripJobs is a customer relationship management (CRM) and business automation software designed specifically for contractors, including painting businesses. It helps streamline communication with clients, automate job scheduling, and manage leads efficiently.

DripJobs also features tools for creating estimates, sending invoices, and tracking payments, making it easier to manage your painting business and keep projects organized from start to finish. For more information, you can visit their website at **www.dripjobs.com**.

Estimate Rocket is an estimating and project management software designed for contractors, including those in the painting industry. It helps businesses create accurate estimates, proposals, and invoices quickly and efficiently. With features for job tracking, customer management, and scheduling, Estimate Rocket allows contractors to streamline their workflow from initial estimate to final payment. The software also offers detailed reporting tools to help track performance and profitability. For more information, you can visit their website at **www.estimaterocket.com**.

Jobber is a comprehensive business management software designed for home service professionals, including painting contractors. It helps streamline tasks like scheduling, client management, invoicing, and payment processing. Jobber also includes tools for creating professional estimates, tracking job progress, and communicating with clients, making it a great all-in-one solution for managing your painting business efficiently. For more information, you can visit their website at **www.getjobber.com**.

Estimates vs. Quotes: What's the Difference?

Did you know that estimates and quotes are often mistaken for the same thing? In reality, they are quite different. An "estimate" is simply an educated guess as to what the project will cost. The final price could be less, or more. A "quotation" or quote, on the other hand, is a legally binding fixed price for a fixed scope of work.

These terms shouldn't be used loosely. Personally, I prefer to send out painting "estimates," not quotations. Why? Over the years, I've learned that issues can arise during a project, making flexibility important when it comes to the final invoice.
In my research, I found that the industry standard estimate-to-job ratio in the home renovation business is 1 to 3.

An Industry Niche. Did you know that the top three professional services hired out by painting contractors are the following:

(1) bookkeepers/accountants,
(2) human resources services
(3) painting business coaches

For every three estimates you provide to customers, you should be landing one job. If you're finding that you're winning every job you estimate, it's a sign that your prices might be too low. Also, keep in mind that if you're frequently offering "free" services or lowering your estimates to compensate for issues, you may be slipping into the "unprofitable" range—which is a serious problem. You never want to operate without making a profit.

In my opinion, consider raising your prices to give yourself more breathing room, and increase your marketing efforts to generate more leads. This way, you may land a slightly lower percentage of jobs but will make better profits on the ones you do secure. Why not try increasing your estimates by 25%? It's something worth considering.

Professionalism, be better than your competition.

Be professional in every aspect of your presentation—this includes not just yourself, but also the condition of your vehicle, your website, and especially your sales materials.

Every detail matters. From staff uniforms to signage, professionalism should be reflected in everything you do. A sloppy or negative company image can seriously impact your business, potentially making or breaking your success.

Always aim to be the best—not necessarily the biggest or the cheapest—but the company known for its quality and consistency. Strive to attract a steady stream of work from a select group of loyal, high-quality clients who value the professionalism and expertise you bring to the table. This reputation will set you apart and ensure long-term success in the painting industry.

When naming and branding your painting business, it's important to invest time and thoughtful consideration right from the start.

As Shakespeare famously said, "A rose by any other name would smell as sweet." In simpler terms, "What's in a name?" When it comes to business, the answer is—quite a lot. Your company name is often the first impression you make on potential customers, and it can significantly impact how memorable and recognizable your brand becomes. With between 175,000 and 260,000 painting companies in North America, standing out in this crowded industry is essential.

For example, in my small city of just 22,000 people, there were 49 different painters advertising their services on Kijiji at one point. Among them, three companies had the exact same first name, four others used the word "Precision," and there were two with strikingly similar names: "Quality Painting" and "Quality Painting Plus." With that kind of overlap, it's no wonder customers can easily become confused or overwhelmed.

To ensure your painting company stands out and is remembered among a sea of competitors, it's critical to invest time in choosing a name that is unique, professional, and reflective of your brand. Your name should not only distinguish you from others but also resonate with the quality and values you bring to your work. Remember, a great name can help create a lasting impression that goes beyond just the services you offer.

Important Business Tip – When choosing a business name, remember that at some point you or a client will need to write it on a check, type it into a Google search, or use it as a website address. A name like "Bobby-Jo's Lake St. Clair Best Painting Company" might not be the best choice. Consider going with something shorter and easier to remember.

Here are six common categories that business owners consider when choosing a name for their painting company:

1. **Memorable Names**
Some choose a unique or catchy name that stands out. Examples include *Hand and Bristle Painting*, *Splatter Painting*, and *Roll with The Punches Painting*.

    - **Pros**: These names are likely to stick in people's minds.

    - **Cons**: They can come across as unprofessional, potentially turning away certain clients.

2. **Names Emphasizing Skill**

    Others opt for names that highlight their expertise, like *A*

Perfect Cut Painting, *Precision Painting*, or *Straight-Line Painting*.

- **Pros**: These names convey a sense of quality and pride in craftsmanship.
- **Cons**: They can set expectations very high, which could backfire if the painter's skills don't match the name.

3. **Owner Names**

Many painters choose to brand their company with their own name, such as *Lockwood Painting*, *John's Painting*, or *Hopkins' Painting*.

- **Pros**: An owner-named company feels personal and trustworthy.
- **Cons**: Clients may expect the owner to personally handle every aspect of the project. What happens when someone else shows up to do the work?

4. **Local Theme Names**

Geographic names are popular, like *Blue Lake Painting*, *Dry Desert Painters*, or *Huron County Fine Finishes*.

- **Pros**: Customers tend to prefer local businesses.
- **Cons**: You might lose clients from areas outside your region, even if you're willing to service them, simply because they don't see you as "local."

5. **Friendly Names**

   A warm, friendly name can build trust, such as *All Care Painting*, *Happy Painting Company*, or *Bright Day Painting*.

   - **Pros**: These names feel approachable and neighborly, which can instill confidence in potential clients.

   - **Cons**: None! These types of names work well across the board.

6. **Money-Saving Names**

   Budget-friendly names like *The Affordable Painters*, *Budget Painting Pros*, or *Painting for Less* appeal to cost-conscious clients.

   - **Pros**: Everyone loves to save money.

   - **Cons**: These names can attract clients looking for rock-bottom prices, which could lead to low-profit jobs and difficult clients.

     Here's a personal story –

     When I first started out, I wanted to draw attention to my services, so I added two simple words to the bottom of my vehicle signage and yard signs: "Quality" and "Affordable." Here's the mistake—using the word "affordable" will attract a lot of "tire-kicking" clients.

These are the clients you want to avoid. Why? They're always looking for the lowest price, are rarely satisfied with your service, and try to add extras at no additional cost. Avoid attracting these types of clients by steering clear of "money-saving" language in your marketing—you'll be glad you did.

The best advice I can give is to combine a variety of positive themes in your branding. People love working with local painters, they want a quality job, and they prefer dealing with friendly professionals. A name that's both local and friendly will always serve you well.

Try to avoid using humorous or unprofessional names. While it might seem popular and attention-grabbing, resist the urge to use words like "affordable," "budget," or "cheaper" in your company name, advertising, or promotional materials. That's the best advice I can offer when it comes to naming and marketing your business.

Our company trailer, vinyl wrapped with our logo and phone number. The website address is listed on the back door. Photo by Carly Martin.

When it comes to branding and choosing a logo for your business, I'd offer the same advice: take your time.

Put careful thought into it before settling on something you might regret later.

Here's another personal story –

During the early to mid-1990s, I worked in the graphic arts and printing industry as a sales representative for a local digital printing company. During that time, I became deeply immersed in graphic design..

I loved everything about it. I even started my own small business doing graphic design work on the side. Fast forward 14 years to when I launched my painting company—naturally, I took it upon myself to design my own logo, business cards, t-shirts, signs, and website.

As I sifted through my graphic design database, I found only one image that seemed acceptable. It was an old-fashioned handyman figure with a bald head, moustache, beard, blue overalls, and a green t-shirt, holding a paint pot and brush.

Here's what my logo looked like pretty much from the start. Simple, with not a lot of clutter. Contact information is prominently displayed.

In In my haste, I put the graphic on my business cards, yard signs, and eventually had the logo wrapped on a utility trailer. One day, my son Lucas asked me what the old guy's name was. I told him he didn't have a name, so Lucas decided to call him Joey. I liked the idea, so I added "Joey" to the logo, just under his foot.

For years, we used Joey in all of our marketing materials. People would often come up to me on the street when they saw me next to the trailer and say, "You don't look anything like the guy pictured on the trailer." It happened so frequently that it really started to annoy me after a while.

At one point, I started telling people that the cartoon was actually of my dad, who looked like that, and that I just worked for him. Of course, it was a complete fabrication, but it ended the conversation quickly.

About seven years later, I decided I didn't like the "Joey" logo anymore. He didn't look like me, he wasn't wearing painter's whites, and he was painting with pink paint—how often do we even do that? I knew it was time for Joey to go, so I began phasing him out of our marketing materials.

I replaced him with a simple paintbrush and can on local phone book ads (*pictured right*). The reaction? People went nuts. The immediate feedback I received really puzzled me.

I didn't think anyone would care what I did with my branding, but I was wrong.

I got emails and phone calls asking, "What happened to the old guy?" and "We really liked the old guy, bring him back!" So, reluctantly, I gave in and brought back the "Joey" logo—and I've kept him around ever since. What I'm trying to say is, take the time to think carefully about how you want to brand your company. Whatever you decide now may stick with you for the long haul.

When it comes to company branding, ensure your logo is simple, memorable, and versatile enough to look professional across all mediums, from business cards to apparel.

The best advice I can offer when it comes to branding, especially in the early stages of your business, is to consider how your logo will appear on various forms of apparel—particularly hats and shirts. Your logo should be simple, clean, and easy to reproduce. The more intricate and detailed it is, the more difficult and costly it can become to print or embroider on clothing.

Think about versatility. Your logo should look great whether it's embroidered on a shirt, printed on a hat, or displayed on business cards and vehicle wraps. Simplicity not only makes it easier to reproduce but also ensures that your branding remains consistent and recognizable across all mediums.

It's also important to explore different production methods, such as digital printing and embroidery, to see what works best for your brand and budget. Why not visit a local apparel shop with your logo ideas? They can offer professional advice on what will look sharp, which materials and methods are best for your needs and provide a cost estimate for producing branded clothing.

Ultimately, investing thought into your branding now will pay off in the long run, ensuring your company logo is professional, memorable, and adaptable for all your marketing needs.

Customer service is important in this business to succeed.

Customer service is important in this business to succeed.

Customer service is important in this business to succeed.

I can't stress this enough. Notice that the title is repeated three times above—I don't want you to miss the point. It's that important. Great customer service will propel you toward success and profitability, while bad customer service will quickly sink you and your company. So, why has my painting business been so successful? Honestly, it all comes down to one thing: customer service.

First, it starts with a friendly voice on the phone. My wife, Valerie, is truly a "customer service expert." Our clients love her and trust her completely. I often hear glowing comments when I'm on a job: "That woman on the phone—the one who came to give the estimate—she's amazing!"

Half the time, they don't even realize she's my wife. Decades ago, when I worked for a cable television company, they introduced me to an interesting business philosophy: always say "yes" to the client whenever possible. While it wasn't always practical, it fostered a very customer-friendly environment. This is something to keep in mind when dealing with your own clients.

Second, my painting staff does everything for our clients. We carefully remove art from the walls, move and protect furniture with plastic, and cover floors with drop sheets. At the end of the job, we sweep and vacuum to leave the space spotless.

If the client requests any small extras, we always accommodate them. We go above and beyond—every time.

That's what every client wants: a hassle-free, exceptional customer service experience. Most clients are willing to pay extra for it, which is something important to remember as you grow your business.

Google Reviews and Customer Service

With the rise of Google Business Listings, which are crucial to the success of your business, having positive reviews has become equally important. One of the first things potential clients will do before contacting you is to check out your Google Business page and read through the reviews.

If you have numerous bad reviews, it can quickly drive customers away. On the other hand, a collection of 5-star reviews will attract clients in droves. That's why it's essential to encourage your satisfied clients to leave you a 5-star review—using a **Google Review Card** can make this process easier and more professional.

If someone leaves a negative review, consider reaching out to them politely and asking what you can do to change their mind. More often than not, a simple conversation can turn the situation around and improve the review.

Always make it a point to respond to every Google review, whether positive or negative. Acknowledging feedback shows potential clients that you are attentive and dedicated to excellent customer service. This personal touch reinforces your commitment to your clients and helps build trust in your brand.

Don't be afraid to ask for help when you need it. If you feel like you could use some guidance, consider hiring a Painting Business Coach. But what exactly is a Painting Business Coach?

Painting Business Coaches are typically experienced professionals who have successfully grown their own painting businesses and now use that expertise to help others do the same. They offer valuable guidance to painting business owners, helping them overcome challenges and achieve their goals. Hiring a Painting Business Coach is like having an experienced partner in your corner.

These coaches provide personalized advice to help you navigate the complexities of running a painting business. This may include setting clear goals, crafting strategies for growth, or developing a plan to revitalize a struggling brand.

Here's another personal story – *Looking back over the past 16 years, when I first started out as a painting contractor, I wish I had access to a painting business coach or an experienced mentor to answer all the questions I had about the business side of running a residential painting company.*

I'm confident that if I had someone to consult with occasionally, those conversations would have saved me from needlessly spending thousands of dollars on ineffective marketing campaigns and advertising.

They would have advised me against buying unnecessary painting equipment that rarely gets used. A Painting Business Coach could have helped me navigate poor project decisions and client interactions, steering me toward better choices instead of costly mistakes.

How can I benefit from hiring a Painting Business Coach?

What makes a Painting Business Coach worth the investment of time, energy, and money? There are many benefits, but here are six of the most important reasons.

1. **Boost your confidence.** The support of a great painting business coach, who gives you encouragement and space to work out challenges on your own, will boost your confidence. It can help you handle conflict, crises, and challenges with greater ease.

2. **Gain some perspective.** We don't know what we don't know. With a fresh set of eyes, and vast experience, a painting business coach can help you see and mitigate your blind spots. They can ask questions that challenge you to think critically and creatively, and act as a sounding board for your ideas.

3. **Leave your comfort zone.** It's easy to fall into the "we've always done it this way" trap. A business coach can push you to try new things, but also help you weigh the risk vs. rewards of a new challenge.

4. **Improve your leadership skills.** Most painting business coaches will offer insights and exercises around personality and leadership styles. By assessing your strengths and weaknesses, you can delegate certain tasks and stay in your zone of genius—all of which will make you a better and more strategic leader.

5. **Boost your productivity.** Doing what you do best, and helping your team do the same, increases efficiency and

morale. That's a recipe for massive productivity gains. Plus, a painting business coach will also hold you accountable for the goals you set, which increases the likelihood you'll meet them.

6. **Make you more money.** A good painting business coach will help you clarify your goals, craft a solid strategy, identify which actions are most likely to increase profits, and hold you accountable for implementation. That usually adds up to more money in the bank.

A recent Painting Contractor Association survey showed that painting business coaches are the second most used professional services by painting contractors today. How can you find one? It's as simple as Googling "Painting Business Coaches" or turning to the last page of this book.

- Notes -

Chapter 2 – Getting The Painting Equipment That You Will Actually Use

Here's a simple list of all the equipment that you will need to start up your residential painting business. A good portion of the equipment that I have bought over the years for my painting company has come from the local hardware store or the paint store.

Some of the specialty equipment like roof hooks, ladder jacks and pitch hoppers that I found available on Amazon or on other online websites.

A two-step painter's ladder. They are a" hard-to-find" item in the hardware store these days, but they can be a valuable ladder to have on hand. They are lightweight and easy to transport. They fit into small closets, and over bathroom toilets. They also fit inside bathtubs making it easier to paint walls and ceilings located in the area around them.

Unfortunately, two-step painter's ladders are no longer legal to use on new home construction sites due to their weight limit of less than 250 pounds, but they are still extremely useful for painting rooms in residential homes. *The average cost is around $60.*

A 6-foot fiberglass step ladder, graded for 250 pounds. Helps you to get to the top of a wall measuring from eight to ten feet in height. *The average cost is around $120.*

 *Here's a quick safety tip for those just starting out with ladders: Always follow the 4-to-1 rule when using an extension ladder. This means the base of the ladder should be placed one foot away from the building for every four feet of height where the ladder rests against the structure.*

Aluminum 16-foot extension ladder, graded for 250 pounds. Helps you to get a maximum height reach of 15 feet. *The average cost is around $250.*

Aluminum 24-foot extension ladder, graded for 250 pounds. Helps you to get to a maximum height of 23 feet. *The average cost is around $279.*

Pivit Ladder Leveling Tool. A wonderful device that helps you with ladder placement on a staircase, a roof pitch or on uneven ground. It is definitely a "must have" tool for any serious painting contractor.

This tool is so helpful on staircases and on roofs. My company owns 7 of them. They also come with a few different accessories. You can get them on Amazon or through your local Sherwin Williams paint store. *The average cost is around $160.*

A 2 foot to 4-foot extension pole. Helps you roll out walls with a height of between eight and ten feet. *The average cost is around $22.*

A 4 foot to 8-foot extension pole. Helps you roll out walls with a height of between ten and twelve feet. *The average cost is around $27.*

A brush extender is a very handy tool for a painter. Using a brush extender mounted on the tip of an extension pole and reach places that you wouldn't be able to with the help of a ladder. *The average cost is around $16.*

A Gooseneck Brush is a bendable painter's brush that you can also mount on an extension pole. Very handy to cut-in those hard-to-reach areas and a real time saver for the painter that has a sharp eye and a steady hand when using it on a pole.

Those painters that can use it to cut in at heights with it without the use of a ladder. I had a chance to meet the inventor of the Gooseneck Brush, Donald Sincennes (pictured upper left) at a Painting Contractors Association Expo. He is a fellow Canadian from Ottawa, Ontario. You can pick up a Goose Neck Brush at Home Depot or find it on Amazon. *The average cost is around $22.*

Paint can opener is a very important painter's tool. Much easier to use than a screwdriver or that random quarter coin that you have in your pocket. Make sure that you have at least two or three on hand because they always get misplaced or end up in someone else's pocket. *The average cost is around $2.*

A 2.5-inch angular sash brush (your choice of brand). Since I started painting, I have been working with either a 2.5-inch or 3-inch angular sash. Many different brands over the years but the model is simply the same. This book cover displays a Lucas Pro Brush (not available anymore). My cost was just over $200.

I'm partial to oval brushes as well. *Average cost really varies depending on the brand you choose. A good brush can range in cost from $5 to $35.*

A Ladder Hook is an awesome tool to use when you need to work outside from a roof with a steep pitch. Ladder hooks are designed to mount on the top of single or extension ladders and then hook over the peak of a roof giving you the ability to climb the steep pitch and paint off the ladder itself. They come with small wheels that help you to mount the ladder and hook together by rolling it up the roof inverted. *The average cost of a pair of ladder hooks is around $70.*

A 9-inch roller cage with a bag of 3/8 inch roller sleeves. I've found that if you keep them clean any roller cage works as well as another. Try to get a contractor bag of roller sleeves if you can, the price point is much better than buying them individually. *The average cost of a single rolling sleeve is around $4. The average cost of a contractor bag of 10 is around $38.*

A paint tray and liners. We love to use the Nour Brand oversized tray and liner that hold an entire gallon of paint. Saves carrying around a cut can when you can empty most of the paint can into the tray and use the paint can itself as a cut can. Just make sure it's completely "shook up" before you do that. Having unmixed color tint in your "cut can" might change the color slightly from the color in your paint tray. *The average tray cost is around $10. The average liner cost is around $3.*

A multi-head screwdriver saves carrying around a bunch of different screwdrivers with you. *The average cost is around $16.*

4x12 canvas drop sheets are much easier to use than having many different sizes. It's good to have around 20 of them available. With that you could cover an area of close to 1000 square feet. *The average cost of a 4'x12' canvas drop sheet is around $19.*

Important Business Tip – *Always use drop sheets. One of the quickest ways to upset a customer is leaving behind paint splatters on their floors, countertops, or furniture after you've finished painting. Even a small mistake can leave a lasting negative impression. To prevent this, always cover surfaces with drop sheets before starting any job. Taking this simple precaution shows professionalism and care, and it will go a long way in ensuring customer satisfaction.*

A Box of painter's plastic is great to have on hand to help protect furniture, kitchen cabinets, ceiling fans, etc. when there is a worry of falling paint splatter. You can always find them where you purchase your paint supplies. *The average cost of a large box of painter's plastic is around $38.*

Sanding Sponge are handy to have when you need to make a surface smooth or to get rid of excess spackling or putty over nail holes or drywall repairs. We always carry a medium/fine sanding sponge giving us options for the amount grit we need for the job. *The average cost of a sanding sponge is around $3.*

Hammer is always handy to have for driving nails or removing nails. You may not always use it, but you'll be happy to have it handy when you need it. Painters don't need anything fancy. A local "Dollar Store" will always have a small, portable hammer at a discount price. *The average cost of a "discount" hammer is around $5.*

Nail Set is an important tool just in case the carpenter doesn't finish his job before you arrive at a job. A spring-loaded nail set would be your best buy. Eliminates the need to carry around a hammer as well. *The average cost of a spring-loaded nail set is around $15.*

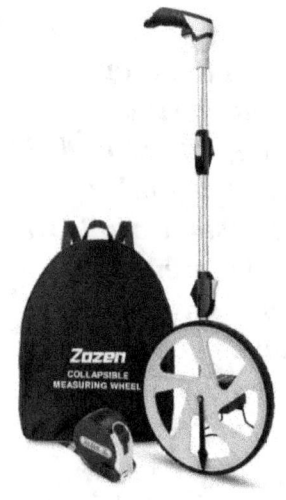

A Measuring Wheel is an important tool to use when doing exterior estimates. You can roll the wheel across the ground as you walk the perimeter of the project. It will tell you how long each wall is. They come in both metric and imperial measurements. *The average cost of a measuring wheel is around $70.*

A Laser Measuring Tool is an important device to make doing interior estimates much quicker and easier. Just "point and click" to get the interior dimensions of a room. Check the reach of the laser beam. They can be anywhere from 35 feet to 100 feet. I use a DeWalt Laser Distance Measurer with a maximum 100-foot beam. Laser Measurers are much faster and easier to carry than using a regular measuring tape. *The average cost of a laser measuring tool is between $35 to $100.*

Tool Tip – Invest in a laser measuring tool that can measure up to 100 feet. While many rooms in standard homes may be smaller, larger homes and commercial projects often feature spaces that exceed 60 feet in length. Having a laser measurer with a longer range ensures you're always prepared for those bigger projects.

Additionally, make sure to keep extra batteries on hand. These devices tend to drain power quickly, and the last thing you want is for your tool to die in the middle of an important measurement. Being prepared with fresh batteries will save you time and keep your workflow uninterrupted.

Green Frog tape is much better than green painter's tape. It's stronger and sticks better. Yes, it's much more expensive, but in a pinch, it outperforms the rest. *The average cost is around $10 a roll.*

A 1.5-inch putty knife is a great tool for scraping down a surface to make it smooth. You can use it for removing wallpaper or for spreading drywall mud or spackling. In a pinch you can also use it as a slot screwdriver or a hammer. *The average cost is around $9.*

A Dripless Caulking Gun and Caulk. A dripless gun would be your best purchase as well as a good elastomeric caulk that is paintable. *The average cost is around $20. The average cost for a tube of caulking can range from $3 to $7.*

A container of spackling (whatever brand you prefer to use) is great for filling nail holes and drywall screw pops. It's easy to work with and sands down well. *The average cost is around $2.*

A bag of assorted rags is always a great thing to have on hand just in case you need to clean up a paint spill or you just need to wipe something. *The average cost is around $25.*

A paint can/bucket hook is a great tool to have when working off a six-foot ladder all day long. Here's a money saving tip – you can always make a paint can hook out of a wire paint can handle instead of buying one. Simply remove the wire handle from the can and bent into a U-shape or an S-shape. The average cost of a manufactured can hook is around $6.

Garbage Bags and Clear Recycling Bags. Always keep a supply of heavy-duty garbage bags and clear recycling bags on hand. These versatile items can be used to wrap up wet paint trays, roller sleeves, and brushes to keep them from drying out between uses. They're also handy for protecting surfaces from splatters if you don't have anything else available. And of course, they serve their primary purpose of helping keep your jobsite neat and tidy by collecting debris and trash.

Clear plastic recycling bags are particularly useful for disposing of empty paint cans, keeping your workspace organized and ready for clean-up. Be sure to invest in contractor-grade bags, with a minimum thickness of 3mm for durability.

The cost of a box of these heavy-duty bags is typically around $35, and it's well worth the investment to ensure your jobsite stays clean and professional.

Wet Paint Signs are great to use in high traffic areas to alert people to the conditions of the surfaces you are painting. Not always foolproof, but at least people can see that you are trying to warn them. The average cost of a sign is $5.

Wire Brush is a great tool for cleaning up your paint brush. After using your favorite brush all day on an exterior painting or staining job, you find that it's caked with paint all around the ferrule.

A wire brush and water are a great way to remove that paint build-up. The average cost of a wire-cleaning brush is around $8.

Titan 440 **Graco 395**

Airless Paint Sprayers. If you're just starting out as a house painter, it's best to start small when investing in equipment. In my professional opinion, the Graco 395 or Titan 440 are ideal choices for beginners. Both models are reasonably priced, durable, and powerful enough to handle small to medium-sized jobs with ease. They offer a great balance between affordability and performance, allowing you to tackle a variety of projects without overcommitting financially.

As your business grows and you take on larger, more complex jobs, you can always upgrade to more advanced models. But for someone just starting out, either of these sprayers will reliably get the job done without breaking the bank. Starting with a well-built, manageable sprayer allows you to get comfortable with the equipment while ensuring you're not overspending in the early stages of your business.

Airless paint sprayers can be a game-changer for your projects, helping you achieve a smoother finish while significantly speeding up the painting process. Popular brands like Graco and Titan offer professional-grade options that are built to withstand the demands of daily use. These professional sprayers can range in price from $1,000 to $10,000, depending on the type of work you're doing and how frequently you'll be using the equipment.

It's important not to confuse DIY homeowner airless sprayers sold at big-box stores like Home Depot with professional-grade sprayers from local paint suppliers. The hardware store versions are typically cheaper because they contain more plastic parts, whereas professional models are made with durable metal components designed to withstand heavy, continuous use. While the lower-cost sprayers might seem appealing, they won't last as long or hold up to the rigors of professional work like the higher-end models.

Investing in a quality airless paint sprayer may seem expensive at first, but it pays off in terms of performance, durability, and long-term reliability. On average, a Graco 395 or Titan 440 will cost around $1,600. It's a good idea to check with your local Sherwin-Williams, PPG, or Benjamin Moore store to find out when they'll be holding a sale on spray equipment. These stores typically have one major sale each year, and taking advantage of it could save you hundreds of dollars.

- Notes -

Chapter 3 – All About Buying Paint. From Whom and How Much?

When I first started my painting business, I immediately began purchasing paint from my local "Color Your World" store. Back in 2008, this chain was corporately owned by the UK-based chemical company Imperial Chemical Industries. Shortly afterward, it was purchased by Akzo-Nobel, which rebranded the stores as **Dulux** in Canada. By 2013, **PPG** acquired Akzo-Nobel's North American operations.

Akzo-Nobel just happens to be the third-largest paint manufacturer in the world, after **Sherwin-Williams** and **PPG**. One of the benefits of buying from corporately owned stores is the substantial discounts they can offer on paint products. These discounts are typically structured around your company's purchase volume: the more paint you buy, the deeper the discount they offer.

For example, after my first five years in business and consistently purchasing around 80% of my residential paint supplies from Dulux, I was paying roughly $38 per gallon for mid-range interior eggshell paint. At the time, I thought this was a pretty good deal, considering the retail price was about 30% higher—around $50 per gallon.

However, my perspective changed when we subcontracted for one of Canada's largest painting contractors. While picking up paint for that job, I received a receipt from the store manager, which happened to include the larger company's pricing. To my surprise, I saw they were paying around 60% less for the same paint I had been buying.

Of course, given their scale, they were purchasing far more paint than my small company, but it still made me think about just how much margin is built into those paint prices. It also raised the question of how much a gallon of paint actually costs to manufacture.

When it comes to franchise-owned stores, like Benjamin Moore, discounts tend to be more standardized across the board, with less variation based on your volume. For instance, despite my company purchasing over $150,000 in paint products annually from various Benjamin Moore franchises in our area, we only receive around a 25% discount on primers, paints, and most sundries.

On the other hand, hardware store brands, like Behr from Home Depot, offer little to no discount for painting contractors. Any savings are usually offered through free product promotions or incentive programs, and even then, I was lucky to receive a 10% discount. That said, Home Depot does put on some great Contractor Appreciation Events, where they give out lots of free swag for contractors and their teams. You can contact the Contractor Desk at your local store to find out when the next event will be.

Geography plays a significant role in determining where we source our paint. My company serves a large geographic area—roughly double the size of Rhode Island but with only one-sixth the population. In this area, we have just two corporate paint stores: one Sherwin-Williams and one Dulux (PPG).

The rest of the area is serviced by eight franchised Benjamin Moore stores. Given the ease of access to Benjamin Moore products, it only makes sense for us to use them. Plus, let's not forget—they make excellent paint.

Industry Niche – Did you know that a recent survey of professional painting contractors revealed some interesting insights about paint purchasing habits? According to the survey, 83% of painters buy their paint from Sherwin-Williams, while 61% purchase from Benjamin Moore. About 24% of painters reported buying paint from PPG, and only 11% said they use Behr paint.

It's important to note that this survey allowed respondents to select multiple paint brands, indicating that many contractors purchase from more than one supplier based on factors such as project requirements, product availability, and pricing.

- Notes -

Chapter 4 – Marketing Strategies
What works and what doesn't work for painting companies?

A marketing strategy for a painting company isn't much different from marketing luxury goods, like expensive jewelry. Painting services are often considered a luxury, much like a Rolex watch or a diamond ring. Because of this, your marketing strategy needs to be carefully tailored to resonate with your ideal customer and have the greatest impact.

So, who is your ideal customer? Simply put, it's individuals or households with a higher-than-average income who can afford to invest in your services. These clients aren't just looking for the cheapest option—they value quality, attention to detail, and professionalism, and they're willing to pay for it.

Your marketing should reflect this. Focus on highlighting the premium value of your work, your expertise, and the high-quality results you deliver. Whether through well-designed digital campaigns, elegant brochures, or a professional website, the key is to position your painting services as an investment in their home, not just a simple commodity.

Brandon Pierpont from Painter Marketing Pros has written a couple of must-read books on the subject. The first one, "The Sales System Playbook for Painting Contractors," covers essential marketing strategies for the digital aspects of your business, including your website and social media marketing.

Brandon Pierpont's *second book, "Painting Millions," is a question-and-answer style guide filled with in-depth interviews and valuable insights from some of the most successful painting company owners today. Not only is it an interesting read, but it's also highly informative, offering actionable advice straight from industry leaders. Both of Pierpont's books are available for purchase on Amazon.*

Marketing Strategies - What works

What Works

Let's begin this chapter by discussing the marketing strategies that, in my experience, have truly worked for my painting company over the years. Keep in mind that things change over time. I've seen many effective marketing methods come and go. It's important to remember this when choosing how to deliver your company's message.

Community bulletin boards are often overlooked in local marketing strategies. These boards, commonly found in busy grocery stores, coffee shops, restaurants, and corner stores. They attract a diverse range of people, offering a broad audience for your business. Make sure to target bulletin boards in areas with high foot traffic. Your flyer or business card should be eye-catching and clearly communicate the painting services you offer. Consider adding a QR code to make it easy for potential clients to contact you instantly.

Paint Store Card Racks are an easy and free spot to market your painting company. Some residential clients just come into a paint store looking for painting contractor referrals. Having your business cards prominently displayed on their rack is never a bad idea. It's a great way to attract more work.

A screenshot of our company Google Business Listing Page.

Google Business Listing is a free, easy-to-use tool that allows painting businesses to manage their online presence across Google platforms, including Google Search and Google Maps. I strongly recommend that you claim and verify your business listing as soon as possible to start leveraging it for lead generation. The more you engage with your listing, the more Google will prioritize showing your business to potential customers.

To maximize your visibility, regularly update your listing with photos of your work, along with daily or weekly posts highlighting your services, promotions, or recent projects. Consistent activity not only boosts your ranking but also helps establish credibility and trust with potential clients.

Social Media Business Listings – Platforms like **Facebook** and **Instagram** offer free business listings that are easy to set up and maintain. These listings provide an excellent way to generate sales leads and showcase your work to a broad audience. Social media platforms allow you to engage directly with potential clients, share updates, post photos of recent projects, and even run targeted ads to reach your ideal customer base.

Never overlook a free marketing opportunity. Utilizing these listings can help you build brand awareness, foster trust, and drive new business without the need for costly advertising. The more active and consistent you are, the more visible your business will be to potential clients.

A screenshot of our business page on Facebook. Notice the phone number.

Facebook Marketplace Classified Ads – In addition to offering a free business listing, Facebook has numerous local-based classified pages where you can advertise your painting services. These community-driven pages are an excellent way to reach potential clients in your area without spending money on traditional advertising.

To make it even easier for people to contact you, consider including your phone number directly in your company name on Facebook. This small detail ensures your contact information is always visible—whether it's in your posts, when your business is tagged in a post, or right at the top of your business page. It streamlines the process for potential clients and increases the likelihood of them reaching out.

Using local Facebook Marketplace ads alongside your business listing will help expand your reach and generate more leads, all while taking advantage of free marketing tools Facebook provides.

Reference Letters – Always make a point to ask your clients for reference letters. These testimonials can be a powerful marketing tool for your painting business. I personally include them in my sales presentation packages and feature them on our website to help build trust with potential residential painting clients.

Trust is one of the most crucial factors when selling painting services. Prospective clients want to feel confident that they're hiring a reliable, skilled professional. If they see that past clients have trusted you and were highly satisfied with the results, they'll be much more likely to take a chance and hire you as well. Reference letters provide real, relatable proof that you deliver quality work and excellent customer service.

Incorporating these letters into your marketing materials can set you apart from competitors and reinforce the credibility of your business, making it easier for potential clients to trust you with their homes.

*Pat and Sarah tacking up a jobsite sign.
Photo taken by Jeff Lockwood*

Yard Signs are an inexpensive and effective way to let homeowners in a neighborhood know that you're open for business and looking for more painting work. They also serve as a subtle endorsement, showing potential clients that you've already done business with one of their neighbors, which can build trust and credibility.

Consider getting some signs printed at your local sign shop. In some cases, your paint suppliers might even sponsor your signs if their logo is prominently displayed. Don't hesitate to ask about sponsorship opportunities. When I first started out, I paid around $30 for a double-sided, full-color sign with a metal lawn stand. Nowadays, you can get them much cheaper. Outdoor signs are incredibly easy to use—once you've completed a job, simply ask your client for permission to place a sign on their front lawn for a week or two. Most homeowners are more than happy to oblige, as long as you pick it up after the agreed time.

You'd be surprised by how many calls you can receive from neighbors who are also looking to have painting done. For a more affordable option, we now order our lawn signs from Vistaprint.com for around $8 per sign.

Here's an Important Tip for Designing Yard Signs – *When designing your yard signs, keep them simple and uncluttered. Avoid overwhelming potential customers with too much information. Stick to the essentials: your company name or logo, phone number, and website. That's often all you need to make an impact.*

Make sure the lettering is large and bold enough to be easily read by people driving past at 30 miles per hour. Clarity is key—if potential clients can't quickly catch your information, the sign won't serve its purpose. Use contrasting colors to ensure your text stands out, and always prioritize readability over fancy design elements. Remember, the goal is to make your contact information visible and memorable in just a glance.

Above are two examples of door hangers I've used over the years. The first one pictured I created in 2009, the second one we had made in 2024. Photos taken by Jeff Lockwood

Door Hangers are an incredibly cost-effective and easy way to let homeowners in target neighborhoods know that you're actively looking for residential painting work. In fact, they provide one of the best returns on investment (ROI) when it comes to marketing your painting business.

When I first started out on my own, I discovered that door hangers were a fantastic tool for keeping myself and my painting crew busy between contracts. They allow you to reach potential clients directly, right at their doorstep, without the need for expensive ad campaigns or digital strategies.

The average cost per door hanger is about 25 cents, making them an affordable way to market your services. We typically order a minimum of 5,000 at a time from Vistaprint, ensuring we always have a steady supply ready for distribution.

Whether you're looking to fill gaps in your schedule or expand your client base, door hangers can deliver an excellent return by generating local leads and keeping your name top of mind with potential customers.

Important Business Tip – When distributing your door hangers, focus on housing developments and neighborhoods where homeowners have an above-average income (around $80K) to a high income level ($200K+). These are the households that will be more likely to afford and invest in your painting services.

In my experience, the success rate with door hangers tends to be about 1 job for every 200 door hangers distributed. This makes door hangers an efficient and reliable marketing tool. You can easily deliver 200 door hangers in just a couple of hours, depending on the walking distance between homes. It's a simple, time-effective way to get your business in front of potential clients in desirable neighborhoods.

The key is consistency—regularly distributing door hangers in your target areas increases your visibility and the likelihood of landing new jobs.

The backside of our business cards, displaying our company "Best of the Best" awards. Unless you hand out a lot of cards, dates make them obsolete quicker than you would think. Photo taken by Jeff Lockwood.

 *Important Marketing Tip – Never print prices or dates on your marketing materials unless you plan to distribute them immediately. Doing so can limit the longevity of your materials and make them outdated quickly..*

Looking back at the previous photos of our door hangers, our first batch was printed in 2009. We ordered a run of 5,000, and on the front, we had a "one room deal for $249" prominently displayed.

Back then, when work was slow and we had days without a painting contract, the whole crew and I would hit the neighborhoods, going door to door and hanging them on front doors. Over the course of a few weeks, we managed to distribute a little more than half the batch.

However, by the time we were ready to distribute more, we got very busy again. When we finally got around to needing them, a whole year had passed, the special pricing was no longer relevant, and the remaining cards were essentially useless.

I made another marketing mistake a few years later. My company won some local "Best of the Best" business awards, and I was so excited that I printed new business cards with the award logos on the back. Unfortunately, the award logos included the year we won, and as time went on, handing out cards with "2018" on them in 2024 felt outdated and less impressive.

These experiences taught me a valuable marketing lesson: always keep your printed materials current and relevant. Avoid including pricing or dates unless you plan to distribute everything immediately. Otherwise, those materials can quickly become outdated, leading to wasted money.

Refer-A-Friend Cards are a fantastic way to turn happy clients into your best salespeople. At the end of every job, we offer our clients the opportunity to refer a friend or relative to our services. If that referral leads to an estimate, we reward the referring client with a $25 Amazon gift card. It's a simple gesture that helps build relationships and encourages word-of-mouth marketing. Remember, nothing grows a business faster than a satisfied client. You can easily find great layout examples for "refer-a-friend" cards by searching on Google.

Vehicle Signage is another inexpensive way to consistently get the word out about you and your company. We once got a $130K a year client simply because they saw one of my company vans parked in a residential driveway close to one of their job sites, and all it cost me was a $40 vehicle window sticker.

More vehicle lettering is shown here.

We have been providing them with painting services for all their new homes and renovation projects for the last five years. You do the math. They are worth the marketing expense. Again, keep your business information short and to the point. Your company name or logo, phone number, website might be all you need to show.

Vinyl labels are much better than magnetic vehicle signs (pictured above).

Here's a personal story – *When I first started my painting company in 2008, I had an older Ford F-150 truck with a cap over the bed. I thought it would be a great vehicle for the painting company. Winter came and I soon found out it wasn't.*

I went and visited my friend at the local sign printing company and had them print me up some beautiful vehicle magnets (picture on the previous page). When I got the magnets, I immediately put them on the front doors of my truck.

Living in a small community where everyone knows everyone, I quickly learned that friends love to flip your door magnets upside down while you're grocery shopping.

I also discovered that if they didn't reattach them properly, they would fly off once I hit highway speeds—and I wouldn't even notice until it was too late.

After replacing missing magnets a few times, I switched to decals, which stay put and don't come off easily. Since then, I've developed a strong dislike for vehicle magnets. Lesson learned.

Real Estate Agents are an excellent source of leads because they talk to homeowners almost daily who need immediate painting work. In my early years as a painter, a couple of local agents sent thousands of dollars' worth of business my way. It's always a good idea to visit your local real estate offices and let them know you're "open for business."

Walk in with a handful of business cards and a box of donuts and coffee. Make friends with whoever's in the office at the time. Offer to sponsor lunch for the next "agent-only" house showing, and some agents may even let you network with others during the event. These private showings are exclusively for agents and can be a fantastic way to meet a lot of local agents from various brokerages all at once.

Here's an important piece of advice when dealing with real estate agents – make sure you treat them right and make sure you compensate them, in some way, for sending painting clients to you.

I know that in some states and provinces that it's illegal to pay them for painting referrals, but I'm sure dropping a hardware store gift card or a gift certificate from their favorite restaurant on their desk would mean something to them and show them your appreciation for their help.

Our local Home Décor Magazines have always been a successful advertising vehicle for us, consistently generating quality leads. Clients frequently mention that they discovered us through the magazine, which is widely read by homeowners looking to make improvements to their residences.

Another advantage is the other advertisers in the magazine, including local home builders, interior designers, and real estate agents, which adds further credibility and visibility for our business. The average cost for a ¼-page ad is around $600, which has proven to be a worthwhile investment.

Google Pay-Per-Click (PPC) Ads may seem expensive at first, but they are highly effective in driving traffic to your website and making your phone ring. Studies show that PPC ads work particularly well in small rural areas, where the cost per lead typically ranges from $35 to $45.

These ads help position your company at the top of search results when potential clients search for "painters near me." While it requires a financial commitment of around $900 per month, the benefits are significant.

One major advantage of Google PPC ads is that you can easily turn them on or off at any time. You can also track their performance with just a few taps on your smartphone. After we began using Google PPC ads, our phone started ringing nonstop. When asked how they heard about us, nearly every new client responded, "Google."

Fun Fact – A recent marketing survey showed that 68% of respondents said that they would pay more money for a service that had a Google Review that strongly indicated great customer service.

Your Company Website – Having a functional, well-designed company website is crucial to your marketing efforts. It serves as the central hub for your online presence, connecting all your digital marketing tools, including your Google Business page, Google Pay-Per-Click (PPC) ads, and your social media platforms like Facebook, Instagram, LinkedIn, Kijiji, and Yelp. Your website is often the first impression potential clients will have of your business, so it's important to make sure it's professional, easy to navigate, and reflects the quality of your work. One key tip: use original photos of your projects, not stock images from the internet. People can quickly spot stock photos, and using real images from your completed jobs adds authenticity and builds trust with potential clients.

Additionally, make sure your website functions well on mobile devices. More than half of website traffic comes from mobile users, so a poorly optimized mobile site can cost you potential business. Ensure that your mobile version looks great, is easy to navigate, and loads quickly—this can often be overlooked but is vital for a positive user experience.

In short, your website is not just a digital brochure—it's a marketing engine that connects all of your online efforts, so it's essential to invest time and care in its design and functionality.

Local Home and Garden Shows – You know your painting services are top-notch, but that won't matter if no one else knows about them. Exhibiting at a local home and garden show is a great way to increase exposure for your painting company and build a stronger brand image that will continuously attract new customers.

These events offer the perfect opportunity to showcase your work, meet potential clients face-to-face, and establish credibility within the community. You can also use the event to boost traffic to your website by sharing links to your site or social media pages with visitors who stop by your booth.

A photo of our booth at a local home & garden show.

If visitors are interested in what you offer, they'll likely visit your website to get a closer look at the full range of painting services you provide. Use your booth's presence to collect prospective clients' information—names, addresses, phone numbers, and email addresses—so you can follow up and stay engaged with them after the show. Offering a prize draw is a great way to encourage attendees to share their contact details. Don't forget to include a QR code on your handouts, leading visitors to an online contact form, your website, social media pages, or an online gallery showcasing completed projects.

This allows potential clients to see examples of your past work and makes it easy for them to connect with you. A home and garden shows are a perfect opportunity to attract new, qualified customers.

While many attendees are already in the market for home improvement services or seeking inspiration, others may remember your painting services when planning their next big project. Exhibiting at these events puts your company in front of interested homeowners, making it easier for them to consider you for their future needs.

Whether you're looking to attract new clients or build relationships with potential business partners, exhibiting at a home and garden show can boost your company's visibility and help you reach your sales and marketing goals.

Marketing Companies for Painters

If you're busy painting and don't have the time to handle all your marketing efforts, there are several specialized marketing companies that can help you run successful campaigns. While these services come with a cost, they are highly effective at generating leads and keeping your painting business busy.

Here are three of the best marketing companies for painters:

1. **Forward Media Marketing – Lucas Jensen**

   Forward Media Marketing specializes in digital marketing strategies specifically for the painting industry. They focus on creating tailored solutions to help painters generate more leads, improve online visibility, and grow their business. With a focus on website optimization, social media advertising, and lead generation, Forward Media Marketing helps Canadian painting companies stay competitive in a crowded market.
   Website: www.fwdmediamarketing.com

2. **Painter Marketing Pros – Brandon Pierpont**

   Painter Marketing Pros is a U.S.-based marketing company that exclusively serves painting contractors. Led by Brandon Pierpont, they specialize in creating comprehensive marketing plans that include SEO, Google Ads, and social media marketing to help painters dominate their local markets. Their proven strategies help painters generate more leads, increase their online presence, and

drive consistent business growth.
Website: **www.paintermarketingpros.com**

3. **Base Coat Marketing**

Base Coat Marketing focuses on providing end-to-end marketing solutions for painting contractors. They offer services like website design, SEO optimization, content creation, and lead management, ensuring your business not only attracts potential clients but also converts them into paying customers. Base Coat Marketing is known for its hands-on approach and commitment to helping painters build lasting success in their business.
Website: **www.basecoatmarketing.com**

Hiring a professional marketing company can free you up to focus on what you do best—painting—while ensuring your business continues to grow and thrive.

Displaying our company's business awards at a local home show.

Business Award Contests are an excellent way to gain additional exposure for your painting business. In today's competitive market, it's crucial for companies to stand out and showcase their achievements. But how can you do this amidst all the noise? Winning a business award can offer numerous benefits, from increased visibility and credibility to boosting employee morale. It certainly worked for my painting company in the past.

Here are several ways business award contests can help market your painting business:

1. **Increased Visibility & Brand Recognition**
   Entering business awards can significantly boost your company's visibility and reputation through media coverage and effective social media promotion. This increased exposure can attract new customers and trade partners. Moreover, it can enhance your brand's image, helping to differentiate your business from competitors and giving you a competitive edge in the marketplace.

2. **Enhanced Credibility & Reputation**
   Making it to the short list or winning a business award for your painting services provides industry recognition and validation. This is a powerful marketing tool you can showcase on your website, email signatures, and social media platforms. Awards signal to potential clients that you are a trusted leader in the industry.

3. **Boosted Employee Morale & Talent Attraction**
   Winning a business award can give your employees a significant morale boost. It shows that their hard work and dedication are being recognized and valued, which leads to increased motivation, job satisfaction, and loyalty.

If you're looking to hire new talent, a business award can also help attract top painting professionals who want to work for a company recognized as a leader in its field, allowing you to build a skilled and motivated team.

4. **New Business Opportunities**
Winning a local business award demonstrates credibility and expertise, which can open doors for new business collaborations and painting contracts. It's a win-win for your company, as it not only builds your reputation but can also lead to increased revenue through new partnerships.

5. **Differentiation from Competitors**
Standing out in the marketplace is key to business success, and entering business awards is one way to achieve that. Simply being part of the contest sets you apart, positioning your company as a local success story. Even if you don't win, being associated with a business awards contest enhances your visibility and credibility.

6. **Increased Customer Loyalty & Retention**
Customers want reassurance and trust when choosing a company, and they are more likely to stay loyal to a business recognized as a leader in the industry. Additionally, winning awards can inspire confidence in potential investors and stakeholders, as awards provide third-party validation of your company's success and future growth potential.

Marketing Strategies - What doesn't work

Here's a list of advertising opportunities that often do not consistently generate leads and can sometimes be a complete waste of your money:

Newspaper Classified Ads – When I first started my painting business, I didn't know what marketing strategies worked best. I noticed that another painting company advertised daily in the local city newspaper's classified section, so I decided to do the same. I ran a 30-word classified ad every day for at least four years, spending about $300 per month.

Did I see a return on that investment? Hardly. Over those four years, only one client ever mentioned seeing my ad in the classifieds. In hindsight, it wasn't a wise marketing choice, and I wouldn't recommend this strategy today.

Yellow Pages – There was a time when the Yellow Pages were the gold standard for marketing service companies. But in the last decade, Google has taken over as the top tool for finding local plumbers, carpenters, and painters. At one point, I was spending between $6K and $8K annually for phone book ads, both in print and online, across four different advertising areas.

Nowadays, the Yellow Pages hardly distribute phone directories effectively in my region. In my town, they simply drop a pile of books in the local Post Office foyer. When you mention Yellow Pages to most people, they aren't even aware that a business directory still exists. Outside of the "free" word listing they may offer, which is always welcome, Yellow Pages is no longer a marketing vehicle I would recommend for any painting company. Just my professional opinion.

Fun Fact – Did you know that a dissatisfied customer tells 9 to 15 people about their bad experience dealing with a service company and 13% of dissatisfied customers tell more than 20 people.

Paid Ad Websites like Houzz, Yelp, and Kijiji can drive some traffic to your website, but often not enough to justify the cost of listing your company. Kijiji, for example, was great when it was free, but now that they charge a monthly fee for local listings, I'm not convinced it's worth the investment.

Yes, the cost is under $10 a month, but even at that price, I still don't see enough value to recommend it. In my opinion, it's another online marketing option that doesn't deliver a strong return on investment.

Random Advertising Gimmicks like phone book covers (now obsolete), grocery store and hardware store bags, and golf course ads are other examples of marketing vehicles that typically don't generate meaningful leads. While they may give your brand some exposure, the results are often difficult to track, and these methods can sometimes be quite expensive.

Over the past 15 years, I've adopted the "10-cent rule" when evaluating these types of marketing opportunities. Here's how it works: if a marketing salesperson offers to print your business card on 12,000 shopping bags for $3,000, that breaks down to 25 cents per bag. Since that's 15 cents over my 10-cent rule, I would automatically decline the offer—unless they're willing to drop the price to around 10 cents per bag. Only then would I consider it.

In general, experience has taught me to avoid these types of marketing options altogether. They rarely provide enough value for the cost.

- Notes -

Chapter 5 – Local Networking Opportunities, Worth the investment?

Business and Trade Organizations are excellent places to promote your painting business and can be a valuable source of information and networking opportunities. But are they worth the investment of your time and money?

Local Business Networking International Chapter (BNI)

I had some mild success as a member of this type of networking group. While it was enjoyable—I loved interacting with other members, learning about their businesses, and getting the chance to present my own painting company every 8 weeks—the overall lead generation was relatively low.

The weekly breakfast meetings were fun, but the painting projects I gained didn't generate enough profit to justify the time commitment. In the end, I realized it wasn't worth my mornings, especially since it interfered with efficiently getting my crews organized and supplied for the day.

Local Home Builders Associations

On the other hand, being an active member of local home builder's associations has been highly beneficial for my business. When I say "active," I mean attending every dinner meeting and special event, and more importantly, networking strategically with members who could become valuable clients. This effort paid off tremendously.

Since joining two local home builders and trades associations, we've gained numerous home builders and renovators as regular clients, adding roughly $450K in sales within just a few short years.

Yes, membership fees can be steep for a small business, but I've found the investment to be more than worth it. Being part of these associations not only brought in significant business but also boosted my company's image and provided prestigious brand recognition within the community. Homeowners take notice when your company is associated with respected industry organizations.

Don't forget to leverage this credibility—display the association's logo on your vehicles, business cards, flyers, website, and social media.

I highly recommend researching your local home builders and trade associations to see if joining would be a good fit for your company. Just remember, you must work at it. Simply being listed in the membership directory won't accomplish much. Attend meetings, network at events, and introduce your company. I send members a marketing postcard twice a year to keep my company top of mind. It really works.

Local Chamber of Commerce

Becoming a member of the local Chamber of Commerce didn't work as well for my company. Over the past 15 years, I've joined two of the largest chambers in my sales area, but I didn't see significant leads or business from the memberships.
In all honesty, it was probably my own lack of effort in networking with the diverse group of members that held me back. Joining a Chamber of Commerce requires active participation to really see results. Hopefully, with more effort, you may have better success than I did.

Painting Contractors Association (PCA)

The **Painting Contractors Association (PCA)**, however, has been an invaluable source of education and support for me and my company. As you've likely noticed throughout this book, I'm a big believer in continuing education, and in my opinion, joining PCA is a must for any serious painting contractor.

The PCA hosts an annual **PCA Expo** and various training seminars throughout the year. Additionally, they hold regular local chapter meetings, often referred to as "local gathering groups," where painters can connect and learn from each other. I strongly encourage you to search for a chapter near you.

The PCA website is also filled with informative videos and articles covering all aspects of the painting industry. I highly recommend joining PCA to take advantage of the wealth of knowledge available. If nothing else, explore their resources and see for yourself how membership can benefit your company. I'm confident you'll find it well worth the investment.

Website: www.pcapainted.org

- Notes -

Chapter 6 - Pricing Jobs – What's the Best Way, The Easiest Way?

Two excellent books to read on pricing painting jobs are both by Pete Wilkinson. His Fast & Flawless series, which includes four books, is a must-read for painting business owners. The first book covers airless spraying, the second focuses on painting systems, and the other two delve into estimating and pricing.

These two titles, "Fast & Flawless Pricing" and "Fast & Flawless Pricing 2," provide invaluable insights into pricing strategies that can help you run a more profitable painting business. Both books are a fascinating read, diving into the reasons why painters do what they do when they first start out in business. I would really suggest that you find them on Amazon and purchase them if you are serious about growing your painting business successfully. Also, the personal stories in both books are interesting and inspiring.

Dennis Gleason is another author who provides in-depth knowledge about estimating painting projects. His classic book, *"Estimating Painting Costs,"* explores the intricacies of painting expenses and offers valuable insights into proper estimating techniques.

In addition, his series of rate books, *"The National Painting Cost Estimator,"* is updated annually and is an excellent resource for painting professionals. Both books are available on Amazon and are highly recommended for anyone looking to improve their estimating skills.

Another valuable resource is **The Painting Contractors Association's** *"The Cost & Estimating Guide, Volume II: Rates and Tables,"* which provides similar production rate numbers for all types of residential and commercial painting projects. It's worth purchasing and is available for download or as a hard copy at **www.pcapainted.org**.

No matter what type of painting work you're estimating or what your specific costs are, I hope my pricing formulas will help you establish rates that consistently result in reliable and profitable estimates.

As Pete Wilkinson wisely said, *"Unfortunately, your painting skills won't make up for your lack of pricing skills."* That couldn't be truer. Knowing how to price jobs effectively is essential for the success of your painting business.
With that in mind, here is my easy strategy and formula for creating your own painting rates, customized to your specific geographic area in North America.

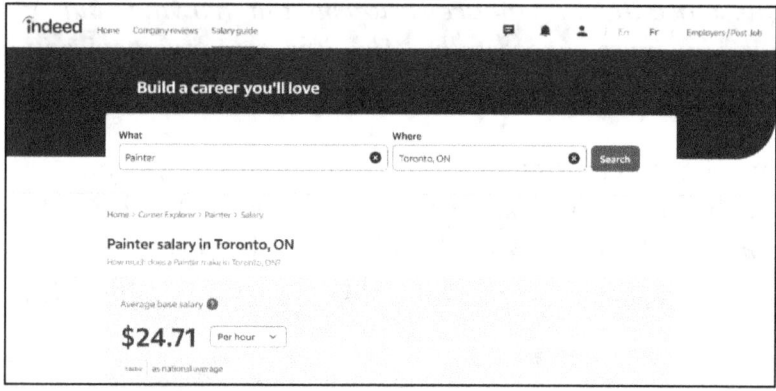

Indeed.com tells me the average Toronto hourly painter's rate of pay is $24.71 per hour.

Step One – Start with the Basics

To begin, you need to determine the average painter's wage for your geographic area. A great resource for this information is Indeed.com, which you might already be using to find painting staff. Simply go to the website, click on "Salary Guide," then type "painter" in the "Job Title" box and enter your location in the "Where" box.

Alternatively, you can ask Google directly. When I refer to the "average painter's wage," I mean the hourly wage of a painter employed by a painting company. For example, let's say you search for the average painter's wage in Toronto, Ontario, Canada, and it comes up as $24.71 per hour.

Now, let's apply my pricing formula.

Step Two – Multiply by 2

Take the average wage you found and multiply it by 2.
$24.71 x 2 = $49.42

Step Three – Add 30% for Business Expenses

Next, add 30% to cover your business expenses, which include vehicle repairs, gas, insurance, marketing, accounting, office supplies, employee costs, etc. This ensures your operating expenses aren't eating into your wage.

$49.42 x 1.30 = $64.25 per hour

This gives you a solid hourly rate for a painting company in Toronto if charging on an hourly basis. Now, let's break it down further.

Step Four – Calculate Your "Day Rate"

Now, let's calculate a minimum "day rate" for one painter working for your company.

$64.25/hour x 8 hours = $514 per day

With this day rate, if a client calls and asks for a small job, like painting a front door, you can confidently respond, "We have a minimum day rate of $514 plus materials. Does that work for you?" You'd be surprised how often clients accept this rate immediately.

Step Five – Determine Square Footage Costs

Next, let's create some square footage numbers to make estimating even easier. Using the hourly rate of $64.25, and based on years of experience, I know my team can paint 1,000 square feet of ceilings, walls, trim, and doors in roughly 86 hours.

Now, multiply your hourly rate by the estimated hours:
$64.25 x 86 hours = $5525.50 plus materials

Materials typically account for 10% to 15% of the total project cost. For this example, we'll use 15%:

$5525.50 x 0.15 = $828.83 for materials

The total project cost is:

$5525.50 + $828.83 = $6354.33

This means that for a 1,000-square-foot space, the labor and materials cost to the customer is roughly $6354.33, which includes paint and sundries.

Breaking that down, it's about $6.35 per square foot to paint ceilings, walls, trim, and doors.

For example, to paint the ceilings, walls, trim, and doors in a 12' x 12' bedroom (144 square feet) would cost approximately:

144 square feet x $6.35 = $914.40

Does that make sense?

Step Six – Use These Square Footage Rates

Using the same numbers, here's a breakdown of costs for pricing by area:

- Ceilings: $2.12 per square foot
- Walls: $4.24 per square foot
- Trim & Doors: $2.12 per linear foot (plus materials)

Important Business Tip *– When pricing out individual tasks, always keep your minimum day rate in mind. If your calculations come out lower than expected, adjust the price to your minimum day rate plus materials to ensure you are properly compensated for the small painting project.*

Notice that $6.35 divided by 3 is $2.12. In the case of wall square footage, you always double it when pricing out. This ensures you're still covering your paint and sundries expense at 15%, and if the client only wants the walls painted, you remain close to your minimum daily rate for smaller square footage jobs.

It's crucial to remember that the most accurate paint estimates are always tailored to each specific project. No single estimating system will fit every type of painting work that comes your way. Your estimates should be based on:

- Your and your team's actual productivity rate

- Material costs specific to your location and paint brand
- Calculated labor costs
- Overhead percentage
- Your desired profit margin

All of these factors should be customized to fit your unique painting business model.

While the information in this book provides a helpful framework, it's no substitute for your own best judgment. No one knows your business better than you. My hope is that my pricing strategy and formulas will help you create your own square footage rates and enable you to complete estimates more accurately, cutting down the time from hours to minutes by eliminating the guesswork.

The numbers you generate from my formula should be combined with the square footage you measure on-site. This could be from rooms to be painted, the exterior of a structure, or blueprints provided by a real estate agent or general contractor. Below are some examples to illustrate different types of estimates, including new home construction, residential interior repaints, and residential exterior projects.

Residential Interior Repaint Example

Let's say a client calls asking for a family room that measures 14' x 14', and they want only the ceiling and walls painted.
Using the numbers we previously established for ceilings and walls:

- Total square footage: 14' x 14' = 196 square feet
- Ceiling: 196 sqft x $2.12 = $415.52 (materials included)
- Walls: 196 sqft x $4.24 = $831.04 (materials included)

Total estimate for the project would be $1,246.56.

A painter with at least three years of experience should be able to complete this project within an 8-hour day, earning a wage of $66.24 per hour, while the company makes a 50% profit to cover additional expenses like vehicles, insurance, sundries, marketing, phone bills, and more.

Key Considerations for Pricing

Remember, the price of your services is determined by the demand for those services versus how many other painters are offering the same. Here are a few key takeaways from this chapter:

1. **The market can fluctuate**—the price for your skills may change based on how much work is available.

2. **You need to make a profit, not just a wage**—always price your jobs to ensure profitability.

3. **Know your worth and charge accordingly**—don't undersell your expertise.

4. **Account for inflation**—adjust your pricing by **2% to 5% annually** to keep up with rising costs.

5. **Adjust as needed**—your numbers may vary depending on your overhead, the economic climate, or other factors specific to your business.

Ultimately, you're in business to make a profit, not just to give yourself a job. All successful businesses operate this way. By understanding your costs, knowing your worth, and pricing accordingly, you'll set yourself up for success in the painting industry.

Chapter 7 – I Need Help !! Where can I find skilled painters when I need them?

In his book, *"Starting a Painting Business,"* Stevie Buell emphasizes the importance of always being on the lookout for additional help to keep your business running smoothly and efficiently. He's absolutely right. Just like a professional hockey team has scouts searching for talented players, you should constantly be on the lookout for skilled painters.

Why is this so important? Because having enough staff to complete your painting projects is critical. If you're constantly short-staffed, you'll find yourself turning down jobs—and that's money left on the table. It's far better to have too many painters than not enough. With more painters available, you can take on multiple jobs simultaneously, increasing your revenue more quickly.

Every painting business should be actively searching for its next "rock star" painter if they want to grow both in sales and profit. Your goal is to find that reliable, experienced painter who consistently performs at a high level—something that's often hard to achieve using conventional hiring methods.

Simply put, top-performing painters are what your business needs if you want to be successful and profitable. But how do you find them?

You can start by placing an online advertisement. I've had some mild success using local online employment boards. Another option is advertising for free on platforms like **Indeed.com**.

Indeed can be effective in finding painting help, but without paying for their premium features, the process can be slow. Additionally, you'll likely need to sift through a large number of applications from painters overseas, from countries like India, Africa, the Middle East, and parts of Europe, hoping for an international opportunity.

Since the end of the COVID-19 pandemic, finding experienced painting employees has become almost a full-time job for many companies. Posting "Painter Wanted" ads online doesn't seem to fill job slots quickly enough, and attending local job fairs hasn't produced strong results either.

So, what's the most effective way to find skilled house painters quickly? The answer lies in actively and continuously recruiting—leveraging a combination of online platforms, local networks, and creative hiring strategies to ensure your business never falls short of talent.

 *Here's an important tip regarding hiring – Two important things to always remember when hiring painting employees or subcontractors. Always be looking for more help and always pay them on time.*

What about poaching skilled painters from other local painting companies. Is it ethical?

In the competitive world of painting contracting, finding skilled labor can be a challenge. Many business owners are faced with the dilemma of whether to actively recruit painters from other companies—also known as "poaching." While it may seem like a quick solution to fill your labor needs, the practice raises important ethical questions and concerns about professional boundaries.

The Temptation to Poach

Poaching painters from other companies can be an attractive shortcut, especially in an industry where top talent is essential to maintain high-quality work. Skilled painters with years of experience are highly sought after, and contractors know that hiring an experienced team member can improve job efficiency and customer satisfaction.

However, as tempting as it may be, poaching brings with it ethical dilemmas and the potential to harm professional relationships within the industry. Before engaging in this practice, it's important to consider the broader implications and whether it aligns with your company's values.

The Ethics of Poaching in the Painting Industry

The ethics of poaching largely depend on how it's done. If a painter working for another company approaches you looking for new opportunities or a better working environment, the ethical waters are murkier. In that case, you're not actively "stealing" talent, but rather responding to an individual seeking advancement.

On the other hand, directly reaching out to employees of another painting company with the intent to lure them away is generally seen as unethical. It can be viewed as undermining the stability of another business by stripping away the valuable workers they've invested in training. Here are some key ethical concerns to consider:

1. **Respect for Professional Relationships**: The painting industry, especially in smaller communities, is often tightly knit. Actively poaching employees can strain relationships with other business owners and contractors. These relationships can be vital for referrals, partnerships, or collaboration on larger projects.

2. **Impact on Employees**: Poaching may disrupt the painter's current employment, leaving them in a situation where they've burned bridges with their former employer. This can lead to instability for the employee, especially if the new position doesn't meet their expectations.

3. **Commitment to Fair Competition**: Building a strong team through poaching rather than fostering talent internally can give a business an unfair advantage. Competitors may feel cheated, leading to hostility and a breakdown of fair business practices in the local painting industry.

Business Boundaries That Shouldn't Be Crossed

While recruiting skilled labor is part of running a business, there are some clear boundaries that should not be crossed when it comes to poaching. Here are some important guidelines:

1. **Don't Solicit Employees Directly**: Reaching out to the employees of another company through LinkedIn, cold calls, or even personal connections is generally considered unethical. Instead, focus on attracting talent through legitimate channels like job boards, word of mouth, or industry networking events.

2. **Avoid Making False Promises**: If you do hire someone from another company, it's essential to be transparent about what you're offering. Over-promising on wages, benefits, or opportunities for growth to lure someone in only to under-deliver once they've made the switch can be damaging not only to the individual but also to your reputation.

3. **Be Honest About Where You Found Them**: If a painter from another company approaches you for work, don't hide it. Transparency about the origin of the recruitment helps maintain trust within the industry.

4. **Don't Violate Non-Compete Agreements**: Some painters may be bound by non-compete or non-solicitation agreements with their current employer. Hiring them could lead to legal consequences for both you and the employee. Always check if such agreements exist before offering employment.

5. **Respect Industry Loyalty**: The painting industry thrives on relationships, and loyalty matters. If a painter is known to be loyal to their employer, it may not be ethical to attempt to sway them by offering more money or benefits. A long-term relationship based on trust, rather than quick gains, will serve both businesses and employees better in the long run.

An Alternative Approach: Building a Great Company Culture

Rather than poaching from competitors, focus on building a company culture that attracts painters naturally. When your business is known for fair pay, good benefits, opportunities for advancement, and a healthy work-life balance, painters will seek you out without you needing to target other companies' employees.

Additionally, investing in the training and development of entry-level painters can help you create a pipeline of skilled workers who are loyal to your business. Apprenticeships, ongoing education, and leadership opportunities can foster talent within your company, reducing the need to look externally for skilled help.

Conclusion: Ethics Over Expediency

While poaching skilled painters may seem like a quick solution, it comes with ethical pitfalls and risks damaging relationships within the industry. The best practice is to focus on developing your own talent and creating a workplace that attracts top painters without actively recruiting them from other companies.

Ethical hiring practices, built on respect and transparency, foster long-term success and professional integrity—values that will serve you and your business well over time.

By respecting boundaries, valuing fair competition, and investing in your workforce, you can grow your business in a way that reflects positively on you and the industry as a whole.

How should I attract painters to my painting company using Great Company Culture?

Attracting skilled painters to your painting company through great company culture is one of the most effective and sustainable ways to build a loyal and high-performing team. When your business fosters an environment that values and supports its workers, word spreads quickly, and skilled professionals will seek you out. Here's how you can create and promote a great company culture to attract painters:

1. Offer Competitive Pay and Benefits

- **Pay Fairly and On Time**: Compensation is a primary concern for any painter. Ensure that your pay is competitive within your market and structured in a clear, transparent way. Pay painters on time—this simple action builds trust and reliability.

- **Provide Benefits**: Offering health insurance, retirement plans, or bonuses can set your company apart from competitors. Even small perks, such as paid time off, can make a huge difference.

- **Offer Pay-for-Performance Bonuses**: Reward your team for their hard work. Whether it's bonuses for completing jobs ahead of schedule, referral bonuses, or a share of profits on large projects, incentives motivate people to perform at their best.

2. Invest in Training and Career Development

- **Training Programs**: Offer training and skill development opportunities to help painters advance in their careers. Investing in employees' growth shows them that they have a future in your company, making them more likely to stay.

- **Certifications and Specializations**: Help your painters achieve certifications or specialize in certain areas (e.g., faux finishes, wallpaper, spray applications). Having specialized training can boost their career prospects and your business offerings.

- **Leadership and Advancement Opportunities**: Give your painters a clear career path. Offer promotions or leadership roles to employees who show dedication and improvement. This not only attracts painters looking for a long-term home but also motivates current employees to stay and grow with your company.

3. Foster a Positive Work Environment

- **Teamwork and Respect**: Build a workplace where painters feel respected and valued. Encourage open communication, collaboration, and mutual respect among team members. Create a culture where everyone feels heard and supported.

- **Provide the Right Tools and Equipment**: Give your painters access to high-quality tools and supplies. Working with subpar equipment can be frustrating and dangerous, so providing what they need shows that you care about their safety and productivity.

- **Supportive Leadership**: Practice hands-on, supportive leadership. Be present, approachable, and understanding of the challenges your painters face on the job. When employees feel supported by management, morale and retention improve.

4. Emphasize Work-Life Balance

- **Flexible Schedules**: Consider offering flexible work schedules to allow painters to balance their personal lives with work. Family time is important to many workers, and companies that respect work-life balance are more attractive to employees.

- **Reasonable Workloads**: Avoid overworking your team. Setting realistic job timelines and avoiding unnecessary overtime ensures your painters remain motivated and satisfied.

- **Paid Time Off**: Offer paid vacation or sick leave. Giving your employees time to recharge not only improves their well-being but also increases their loyalty to your company.

5. Promote a Strong Company Vision and Values

- **Clearly Defined Values**: Articulate your company's values and make sure they align with those of your workers. Painters want to work for a company that has a purpose beyond just making money. If your company stands for quality workmanship, integrity, and respect for clients and employees, you will attract like-minded individuals.

- **Involve Employees in Decision-Making**: Show that you value your employees' input by involving them in decisions about work processes, job planning, and company goals. Painters are more likely to feel engaged and loyal when they have a voice in the business.

6. Highlight Job Security and Stability

- **Long-Term Projects**: Painters often look for steady work, not just one-off projects. Offering consistent work or guaranteed contracts can provide job security and make your company more appealing.

- **Focus on Retention**: Show potential hires that your business prioritizes employee retention. Highlight how long your current employees have been with you, which demonstrates that you foster loyalty and stability.

7. Publicize Your Company Culture

- **Use Social Media and Your Website**: Showcase your company culture online. Post about team-building events, employee achievements, and the positive work environment you've created. Prospective painters will see that you offer more than just a job—you offer a place where they'll be valued.

- **Share Testimonials from Current Employees**: Ask your current team members to share their experiences working for your company. Video testimonials or quotes about the supportive environment, career opportunities, and work-life balance can be incredibly persuasive.

- **Advertise Culture on Job Listings**: When advertising job openings, don't just list pay and benefits. Emphasize your company's values, work culture, and what makes it different. Painters who are looking for more than just a paycheck will be drawn to your company.

8. Encourage Employee Engagement and Recognition

- **Employee Recognition Programs**: Regularly recognize and reward excellent work. This could be in the form of 'Painter of the Month' awards, small bonuses for performance, or even public recognition during team meetings. Painters who feel appreciated are more likely to stay and recommend your company to others.

- **Team Building and Social Activities**: Organize regular team-building events or social gatherings to create a sense of camaraderie. A painter is more likely to choose a company where they feel they are part of a supportive and friendly team.

9. Lead by Example

- **Leadership with Integrity**: As the business owner, you set the tone for the entire company. Demonstrate integrity, fairness, and a strong work ethic. Painters will be drawn to a leader who treats them with respect and leads by example.

- **Supportive Environment**: Create an atmosphere where painters feel comfortable sharing concerns, asking for help, or seeking feedback. A positive, open environment leads to higher morale and productivity.

10. Employee Well-Being

- **Focus on Health and Safety**: Make sure your workplace prioritizes health and safety. Painters work in physically demanding conditions, and providing proper protective equipment and ensuring a safe work environment shows you care about their well-being.

- **Mental Health Support**: Painters often work long hours under stressful conditions. Offering resources or support for mental health, such as access to counselors or time off for stress relief, can further demonstrate your commitment to their overall well-being.

Building a great company culture is one of the best ways to attract and retain skilled painters. By creating an environment where your employees feel valued, supported, and motivated, you'll naturally draw in top talent. Painters looking for stability, career growth, and a positive work environment will seek out companies with strong cultures, ultimately making your business more competitive in the industry. Invest in your team's well-being and professional growth, and the results will speak for themselves.

Why not try to hire a few subcontractors to take on your extra painting project workload.

Working with painting subcontractors is another viable option. When it became very hard to hire skilled painters, I turned to hiring other local painting professionals to help me with my workload. Once I figured out how to do it, it was very simple to do. One day I made a point to visit every paint store in my service area and I collected all the painting contractor business cards I could find.

Using the information that I collected from the paint stores I contacted each company individually and asked if they were open to the idea of subcontracting painting work for me and my company. Out of the small group that I contacted only a handful were interested.

I set up interviews for each of them and conducted them just like I would if I was hiring a painting employee for the company.

Always give them an interview, a test and then a painting audition. Just as if you were hiring them as an employee

Every time I conduct an employee interview or when I interview a subcontractor I take them through the same process. I have them fill out a standard employee application. It shows me that they can follow instruction, helps me to discover whether they can read and write. Let's me know whether they have a criminal record or not and I have them sign the bottom. Wording on the application gives me permission to search their social media accounts on Facebook and Instagram, etc.

Next, I ask them directly, "What kind of money are you looking for?" That's an important question. I have them fill out a Subcontractor Information Form and take a "Painter's Quiz" to see how much about the painting industry they know. (see the "Painter's Quiz" in Appendix C at the back of the book).

All this information helps you to make an informed decision about whether or not you would be comfortable with this person representing your company.

Then comes the audition. Do they have the skills necessary to do the job to your professional expectations? The only way to really know is to give them an "audition".

- Notes -

Chapter 8 – My Final Thoughts

Thank you for taking the time to read my book. I sincerely hope that you found some of my business tips and strategies useful as you continue to grow your own painting business.

As a passionate professional painter myself, I believe that every dedicated painter shares the desire to raise the overall standards of the painting industry in North America. One of my personal goals is to see the business side of the trade taught openly, rather than being closely guarded by the most successful contractors. I hope the information in this book provides encouragement to solo painters just starting out, showing that there is indeed a bright future ahead. You can build a rewarding painting career and earn a great living doing what you love.

Before speaking on an expo panel, I was asked to provide an inspirational quote. Here's what I shared with the audience:

> *"Know your worth when pricing out jobs. Build a trusted company image, and sales growth will follow."*

I wish you the best of luck in your painting career and the greatest of successes.

If you'd like to reach out for any further help, feel free to contact me at jeff@paintingbizcoach.com.

Painting Contractor Business Books You Should Buy and Read

I love to read books about the painting business. Education just makes us all better at what we do both painting wise and business wise. I own pretty much every book available on the business side of the painting trade

There aren't a ton of books on the painting business available, but here is a list of painting business books that I have read, and I think you might want to consider reading as well. Almost all these books are available for purchase on Amazon.

The Business of Painting by Arthur Cole – *Last edited in 2012. I did find it a little dated in some spots, but it's still full of great advice and information about the painting business.*

How to Start a Home-Based Painting Business by Deborah Bouziden – *Over 122 pages. It covers lots of business topics from buying equipment to working with a partner.*

Fast and Flawless- A guide to Airless Spraying by Pete Wilkinson – *A great book about the painting business. He explains why a major part of your painting business model should be airless spraying.*

Fast and Flawless Pricing – A guide to pricing and business for decorators by Pete Wilkinson – *Pete dives into why painting businesses fail for the lack of knowing how to price out painting projects.*

Fast and Flawless Pricing 2 – A guide to pricing and business for decorators by Pete Wilkinson – *In this book, Pete tells us why it's so important to not just make a wage but make a profit for your painting company as well.*

Paint Contractor's Business Manual by Kevin McGeer – *Kevin takes you through the basics of the painting business and directs the reader how to make a great living as a painting contractor.*

Crushed it! How I made $7.5 Million as a House Painter & How You Can Too by Terry Begue – *A wonderful read. Terry takes you through his step-by-step process to develop your brand, build trust with customers and prospective clients.*

The Sales System Playbook for Painting Contractors by Brandon Pierpont – *Brandon explains how to build a marketing and sales system for your painting business that works.*

Painting Millions by Brandon Pierpont – *A brilliant book. A written version of in-depth conversations with leading painting contractors. Together they talk about sales, marketing, worst mistakes, partnerships and more.*

At Your Best as a Painter by Juan Carosso – *A step by step guide to a successful career as a painting contractor.*

National Painting Cost Estimator by Dennis Gleason – *a comprehensive rate guide to estimating various types of painting projects. Rates updated yearly.*

Estimating Painting Costs by Dennis Gleason – *a manual detailing the processes associated with painting project estimating including bidding strategies, contracts and financial management.*

Paint Contractor's Manual by Dave Matis and Jobe H. Toole – *a comprehensive manual explaining how to start and run a profitable painting contracting business.*

Painter's Handbook by Bill McElroy – *a complete guide explaining what painters and painting contractors need to know to thrive in the painting contracting business.*

Additional painting contractor resources you should check out are the following -

American Painting Contractor Magazine -
https://www.paintmag.com/american-painting-contractor-magazine

Paintlife Supply – Chris Berry, The Idaho Painter
https://paintlifesupply.com/

Painting Contractor Association –
htttps://www.pcapainted.org

Appendix A

DIY Paint Brush Hanging Bucket

Makes cleaning brushes so much easier. I got the idea for this version while working for the second painting company that I had ever worked for. They were third generation painters and their granddad introduced them to the "hanging bucket".

<u>Hardware Requirements</u> – (1) 5-gallon bucket, (4) 3/8X3" Machine Screws, (4) 3/8" nuts, (8) 3/8 washers. <u>Instructions</u> – (1) drill 4 holes equally distanced around the top edge of the bucket. (2) Insert a machine screw with a washer through a hole on the outside of the bucket. Repeat 3 more times. (3) Thread and tighten a washer and a nut on the inside of each of the machine screws. The whole project costs less than $15 for the materials.

Inside view   Outside view   Complete

Appendix B

Anatomy of a Paint Brush

Something Every Professional Painter Should Know Because We Use Paint Brushes Everyday

I had to include this appendix in the book because I think it is something important that most painters don't know but really need to know. How does a paint brush work? What are its component parts and how do they function? All answered in this appendix that I found online.

To achieve a good quality finish to your paintwork you will need to know the right type of brushes and sizes for different types of paint to produce a good quality finish.

When it comes to workmanship you can within reason blame your brushes, using a poor-quality decorator brush you will find that they will lose their shape and stiffness plus lose filaments as your painting.

Good quality brushes, on the other hand, retain their shape which is important when you are striking a long straight line on skirting boards or glazing bars.

Another advantage is that they hold more paint with less dripping and spattering when you are applying the paint.

Using a good quality brush like badgers' hair will minimize brush marks and a smoother finish especially with oil-based paints and all varnishes.

The quality of the finish will also depend upon the skill of the painter applying the paint.

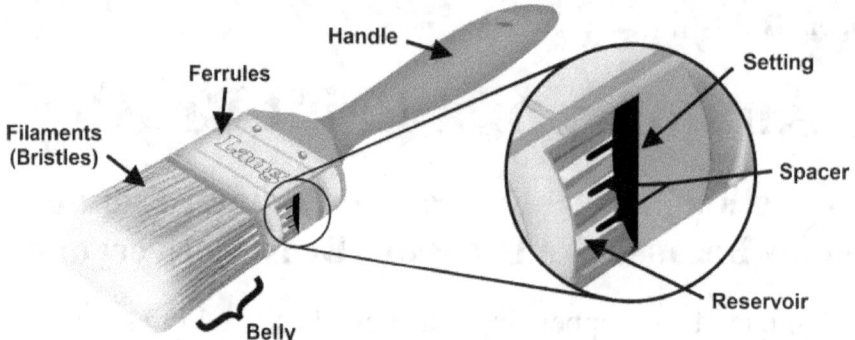

The Handle

Handles come in different shapes and sizes depending upon size and function of the paintbrush, typically made from wood like beach, ash or elm and sealed to make cleaning and handling easier also can be made from plastic.

Ferrule

The ferrule is the metal part between the handle and filaments. This is to secure the filaments to the handle by riveting or by steam jointing to the handle which doesn't need rivets.

Common ferrules are made from nickel-plated metal which will rust when using water-based paints, alternatively, you can purchase copper ferrule which is more expensive.

Pure Bristle

Pure hair bristles come from wild pigs, boars or hogs, they have good strength and flexibility. Pule bristles have four qualities, the flag, serrations, the natural taper and natural springiness.

The **Flag** is split into several strands this provides a softer end, which helps with the laying off process giving you a smoother finish plus minimizing brush marks.

A good painter and decorator normally have two sets of pure bristle brushes, the newest set is used to apply base coats this helps to break in the brush, the older set is used for the final coat for a smoother finish.

Serrations or scales along the length of the bristle help to hold more paint and prevent the bristles from lying too close to each other.

Pule bristles have a **Natural Taper** curving inwards from the root to tip which forms a belly, this is the fattest part of the brush which also acts as a reservoir just like the spaces in the setting.

Each paintbrush contains up to 5 different lengths. This bristle's structure makes the brush sufficiently stiff. Dusting brushes have their bristles reversed when placing into the setting and form a natural curve outward.

Do not use pure bristles when applying water-based paints, the bristles will absorb the water from the paint losing their **Natural Springiness** and splay.

On rough surfaces do not use pure bristles as they will be damaged by the surface, alternative used synthetic brushes will last a lot longer.

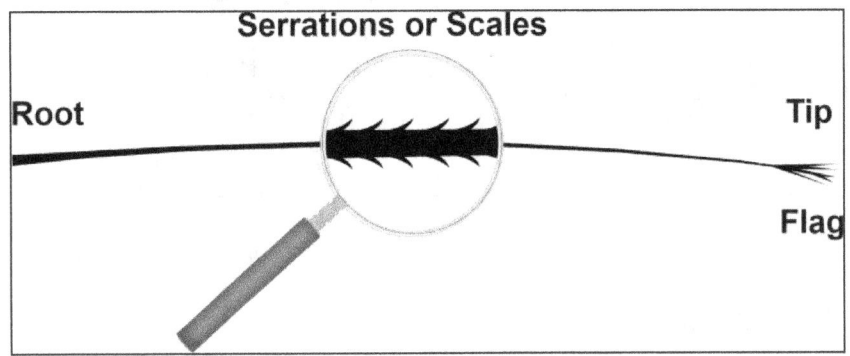

Horsehair

Horsehair is cut from the tail and the manes; the hair has a little spring, and no taper needs to be mechanically split or flagged.

To produce a cheaper and softer brush it is sometimes mixed with bristles, the supplier should clearly state this on the packaging.

Synthetic Brushes

The filaments are made from polyester, nylon, or a mixture of both being the higher quality blend for paintbrushes.

During the manufacturing process, the manufacturers can flag the ends of the bristles which allows the bristles to absorb and hold more paint.

Advantage of synthetic bristle brushes they can apply a wide range of paint types, plus they do not expand when using water-based paints and are easy to clean.

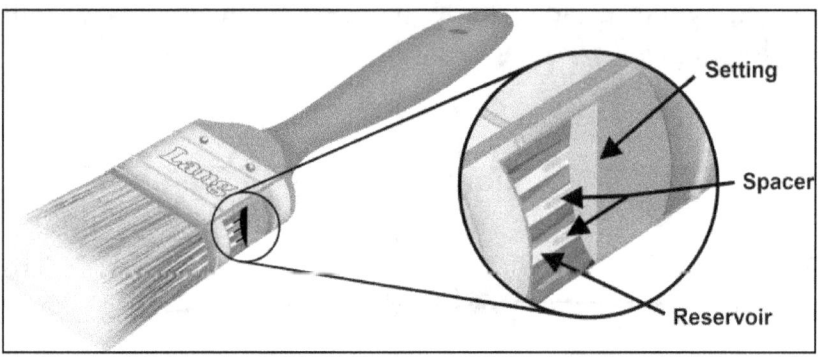

The Setting

The setting is a Synthetic Resin glue all the bristle routes together, manufacturers also use Vulcanized Rubber or Shellac.

Spaces in the setting create a void between the bristles enabling the brush to load more paint inside the reservoir.

IMPORTANT TO NOTE:

Do not use brushes in paints that contain solvents that will dissolve the setting, thus creating bristle loss.

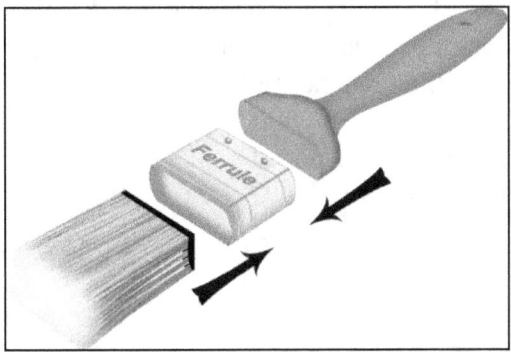

The ferrule is the metal part between the handle and filaments.

Filaments (Bristles) are dipped into the setting; this is heated at temperature to allow curing of the solution (Setting). This is allowed to cool down and set before insertion into the ferrule at this stage the handle is inserted as well.

The whole ferrule is then pressed, seamed or riveted once this is completed the bristles are dipped into a moth-repellent solution.

Appendix C

A PRO PAINTERS QUIZ

How much do you know about the painting trade? Take this painter's quiz and check your knowledge about painting. In this quiz, we have questions about paint products, the techniques of painting, and the terms related to painting and painter's tools.

1. **Can you name the three popular brand names of paint that professional painters use?**

   _____ _____ _____

2. **Can you name five paint sheens?**

   1. _____

   2. _____

   3. _____

   4. _____

5.

_____

3. Price wise, what's cheaper to buy – an oil base primer - or a water-based primer?

4. Can you name 2 types of specialty primers and what situation they are commonly used for?

Name   Name

Special Use   Special Use

5. Circle the photo that demonstrates the proper way a professional painter holds a paint brush. How would you hold a brush when painting?

 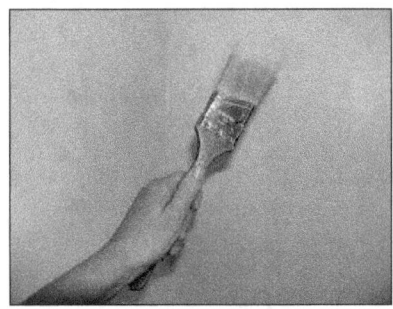

6. **Exterior Vinyl siding can be painted when? Check your answer.**

   ___ A lighter color of acrylic paint is used

   ___ A darker color of acrylic paint is used

   ___ Both a and b   ___ Never

   Why did you choose this answer?

7. **Choose the most common hazard encountered when working as a painter?**

   A. Lead-based paint   B. Toxic fumes

   C. Falling off a ladder   D. Electrical shock

8. **In which order would you complete these tasks to completely repaint a bedroom? Please number from first to last, 1 to 10.**

   _____ Paint the baseboards.

   _____ Paint the doors.

   _____ Paint the window and door trim.

   _____ Fill nail holes.

   _____ Remove switch and plug plates.

_____ Paint the walls.

_____ Repair any cracks in the walls or ceiling.

_____ Paint the ceiling.

_____ Lay down drop sheets. Cover the furniture.

_____ Paint the closet.

9. From preparation thru clean-up, roughly, how long would it take you to completely paint, 2 coats, on just the walls, in a fully furnished bedroom measuring 12'x12'? How many gallons of paint will you need to finish it?

How long? _____

How many gallons? _____

10. About how many square feet does a normal gallon of interior paint cover? Check your answer.

___ 150 to 200 sqft   ___ 250 to 400 sqft

___ 450 to 600 sqft   ___ over 600 sqft

11. Have you ever removed wallpaper before? If yes, which method(s) did you use and why?

12. What sheen is ceiling paint typically?

13. What is the proper way to dispose of paint? Choose one answer.

   __ Pour down the drain, rinse

   __ Seal the container and throw it away

   __ Leave the lid off to dry out and throw it away.

   __ Don't dispose; paint is good forever.

14. What is the most common cause of paint defects? Check your answer.

   ___ Product expires

   ___ Surface preparation

   ___ Weather condition when applied

   ___ The mixture of thinner and base paint

15. Why do painters use drop cloths and plastic? Check your answer.

   ___ Protect flooring and furniture from splatter.

   ___ Protect against spills

   ___ To help avoid tracking paint into other spaces.

   ___ All of the above

16. What is your preferred nap thickness of roller sleeve for a wall-and-ceiling job? Circle your answer and tell us why you chose it.

    3/8-inch (10mm)   ½ inch (13mm)   ¾ Inch (19mm)

    Why? _____

17. For what reason would a pro painter ever ask the paint store to "tint the primer" gray?

18. Why should paint rages with oil-based primer, paint or stain not be left at job sites, especially overnight when it is most likely to be unattended? Check your answer.

___ It will absorb air moisture and dirt to affect the paint quality.

___ Rags can be mistaken for a paintbrush and used for wall painting.

___ It can be mistaken as a trash can and easily be thrown anywhere.

___ The soiled rages might ignite and start fire.

19. **In painting terms, what does it mean to "cut in? Check your answer in the spot below.**

___ Step in front of someone   ___ Mix paint of different colors

___ Remove old caulk   ___ Paint corners and edges

20. **What is your favourite size of brush for "cutting in" and why?**

21. <u>**Anatomy of a Staircase**</u>. **Please number the correct parts of the staircase in the diagram below.**

1 - Inner String   5 – Outer String

2 – Riser   6 – Newel Post

3 – Tread   7 - Baluster

4 – Handrail   8 – Nosing

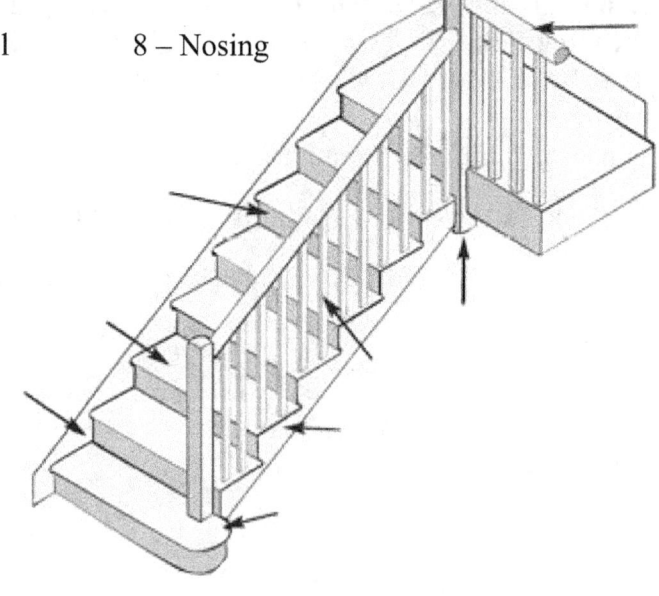

22. Anatomy of a Paint Brush. Name the correct parts of a paint brush in the diagram below.

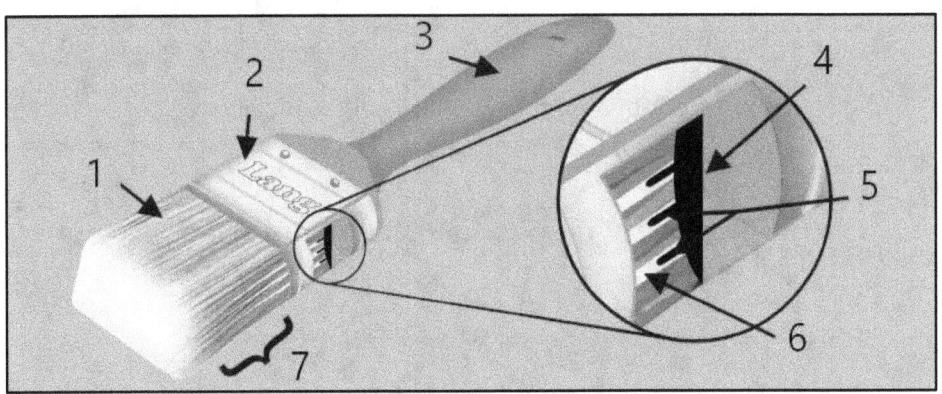

1 – _____

2 – _____

3 – _____

4 – _____

5 – _____

6 – _____

7 - _____

23. What is the purpose of a primer before painting? Circle the correct answer.

A - to seal drywall

B - to cover darker colors

C - To help topcoat to adhere.

D - all of the above

24. Write the name of the painter's tools shown below. Pictures are not to scale –

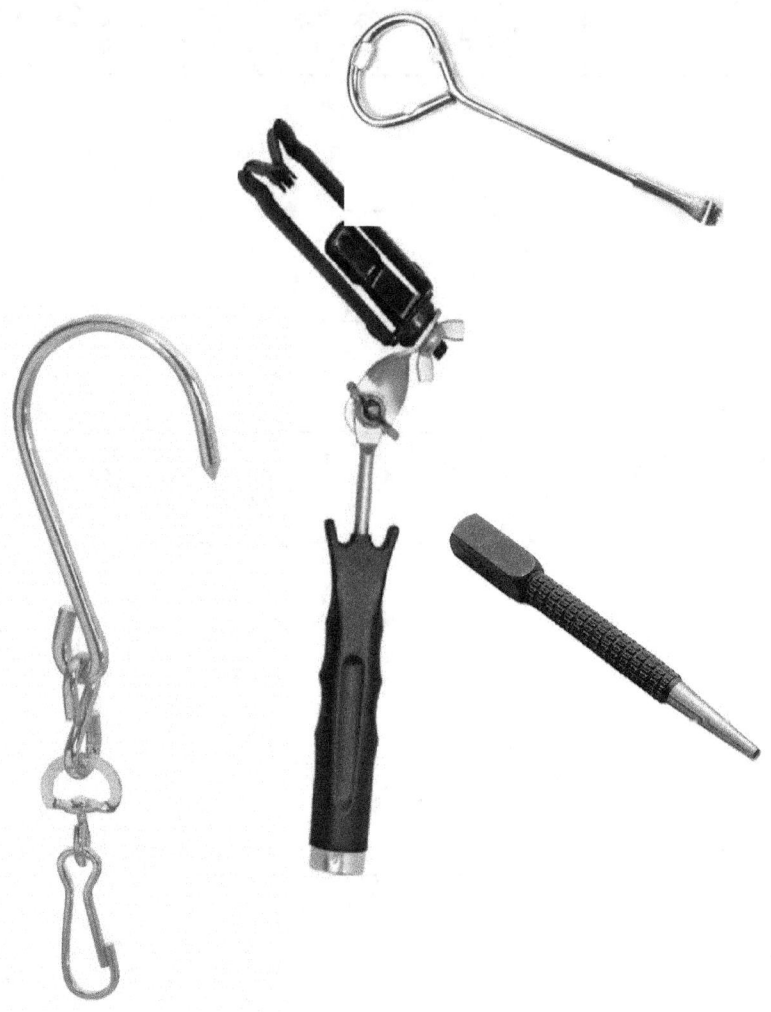

25. At what temperature should the paint be stored?

___ The hotter, the better!   ___ Below freezing

___ Room temperature   ___ It doesn't matter

Your score was _____ out of 25

Rating	1-5	Novice / Beginner
	6-10	DIY Homeowner
	11-15	Apprentice Painter
	16-20	Pro Painter
	21-25	Master Painter/Decorator

Answers

1. Sherwin-Williams, Benjamin Moore, PPG

2. Flat, Matte, Pearl, Satin, Eggshell, Semi-gloss, Gloss

3. Water-based Primer

4. Stix/adherence, BIN/stain blocking

5. First photo is the correct way to hold a brush.

6. Answer is A - A lighter color of acrylic paint is used. Why - Vinyl siding when manufactured is heated rated for the color it was created in. It can only be painted lighter than the original color to be "vinyl safe". This is because lighter colors reflect more light and heat, reducing the risk of the vinyl siding warping or becoming damaged. Darker colors absorb more heat, which can cause the vinyl siding to expand and contract, leading to potential damage. Therefore, always using the same as the original color or a lighter color of acrylic paint is recommended for painting any type of vinyl siding.

7. Answer is C – Falling off a ladder

8. Answers are in the following order - Lay down drop sheets, cover the furniture. Repair any cracks in the walls or ceiling. Fill nail holes. Remove switch and plug plates. Paint the ceiling. Paint the closet. Paint the window and door trim. Paint the walls. Paint the baseboards. Paint the doors.

9. Answer should be close to 5-6 hours and 2 gallons

10. 250 to 400 square feet

11. If yes – steamer, chemical, fabric softener, hot water

12. Flat

13. Leave the lid off to dry out and throw it away

14. Surface preparation

15. All the above

16. Personal preference question.

17. Applying a deep red colour topcoat.

18. The soiled rages might ignite and start fire.

19. Paint corners and edges

20. Personal preference question

21. Staircase Answers

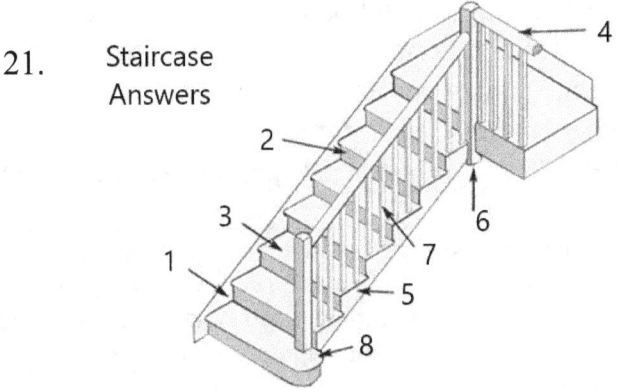

22. (1) Bristles (2) Ferrule (3) Handle (4) Setting (5) Spacer (6) Reservoir (7) Belly

23. All the above

24. Paint Can Hook, Brush Extender, Paint Can Key, Nail Set

25. Room Temperature

Appendix D

AVERAGE PAINTING SQUARE FOOTAGE HOURS

After years of collecting project data, we determined that it takes the average painter a certain amount of time to complete a painting project within a certain amount of square feet. Below are the numbers that we have come up with. I hope you find them as useful as we do when estimating painting projects.

* Approx. hours of labor per square foot in a residential painting project with average preparation plus two coats of paint on ceilings, walls, baseboards, trim and doors. Numbers correlate for a painter(s) with approximately 2000 to 4000 hours of professional residential painting experience.			
100 SQFT	9 HOURS	1600 SQFT	140 HOURS
200 SQFT	18 HOURS	1700 SQFT	148 HOURS
300 SQFT	26 HOURS	1800 SQFT	157 HOURS
400 SQFT	35 HOURS	1900 SQFT	165 HOURS
500 SQFT	44 HOURS	2000 SQFT	174 HOURS
600 SQFT	52 HOURS	2100 SQFT	183 HOURS
700 SQFT	61 HOURS	2200 SQFT	192 HOURS
800 SQFT	70 HOURS	2300 SQFT	200 HOURS
900 SQFT	79 HOURS	2400 SQFT	209 HOURS
1000 SQFT	87 HOURS	2500 SQFT	218 HOURS
1100 SQFT	96 HOURS	2600 SQFT	226 HOURS
1200 SQFT	105 HOURS	2700 SQFT	235 HOURS
1300 SQFT	113 HOURS	2800 SQFT	244 HOURS
1400 SQFT	122 HOURS	2900 SQFT	252 HOURS
1500 SQFT	131 HOURS	3000 SQFT	261 HOURS

** Thanks to Donna-Lea for compiling these numbers.

Appendix E

Various Diagrams of Parts of a House

Useful information when estimating and invoicing to know the exact names of various parts of a house.

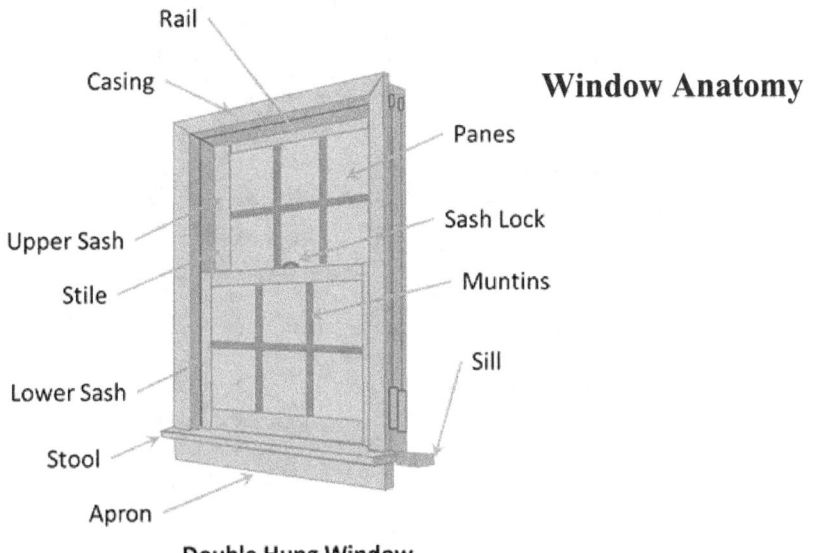

Window Anatomy

Double Hung Window

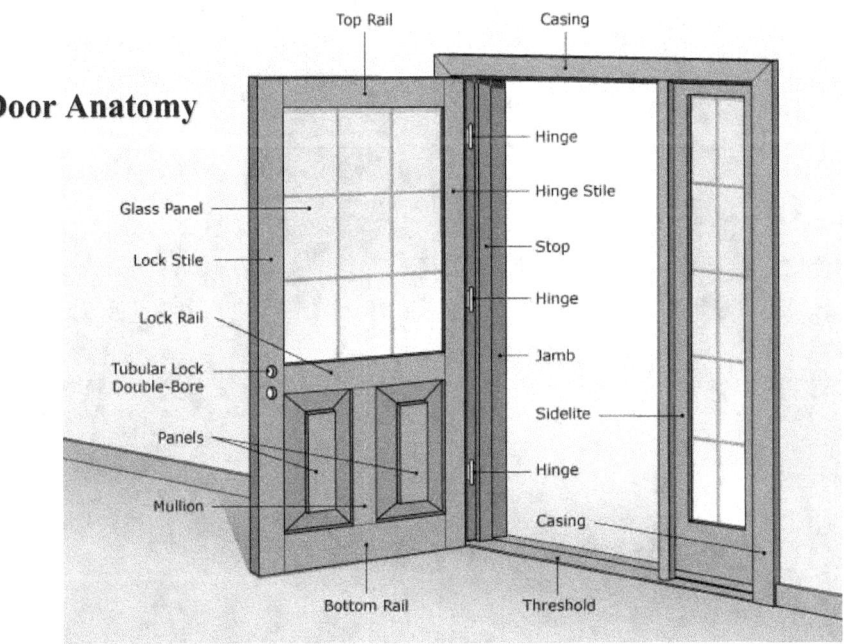

Door Anatomy

Interior Anatomy

Exterior House Anatomy Pt.1

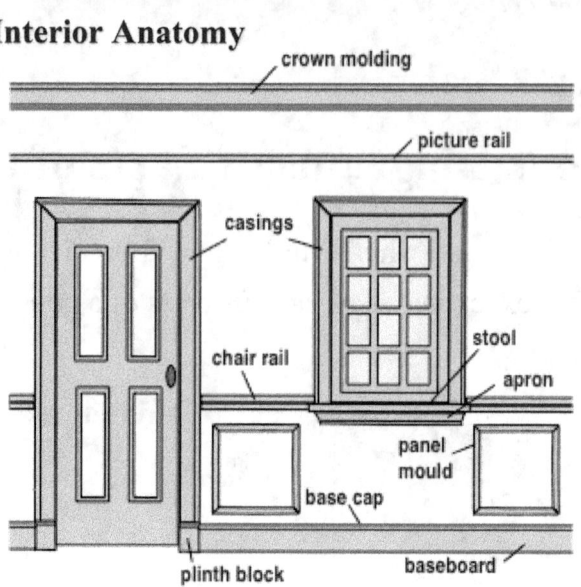

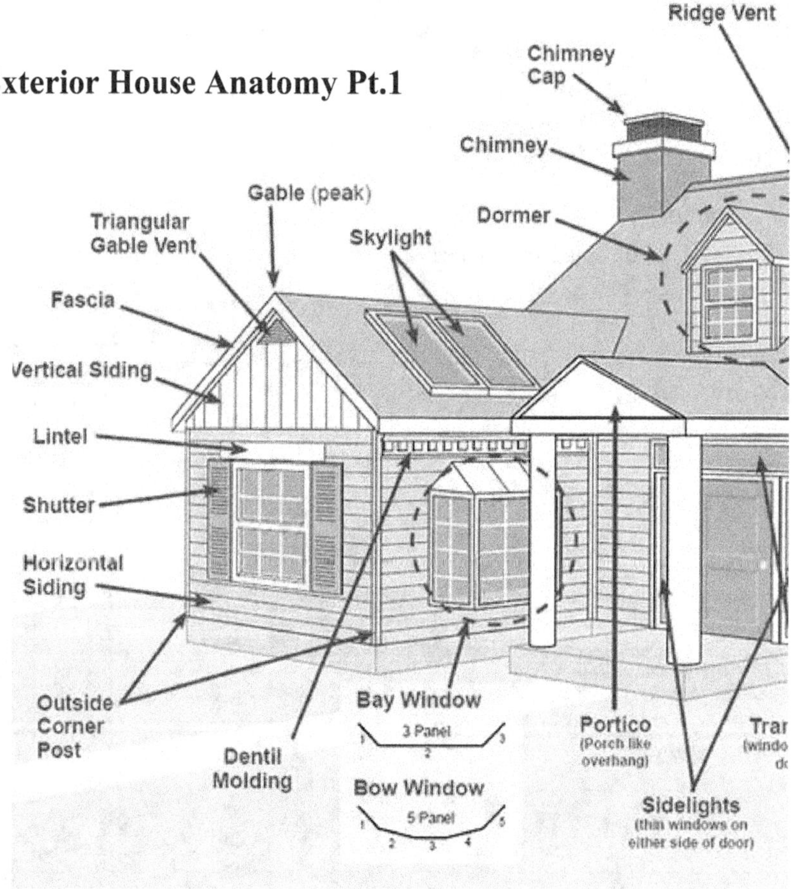

Exterior House Anatomy Pt.2

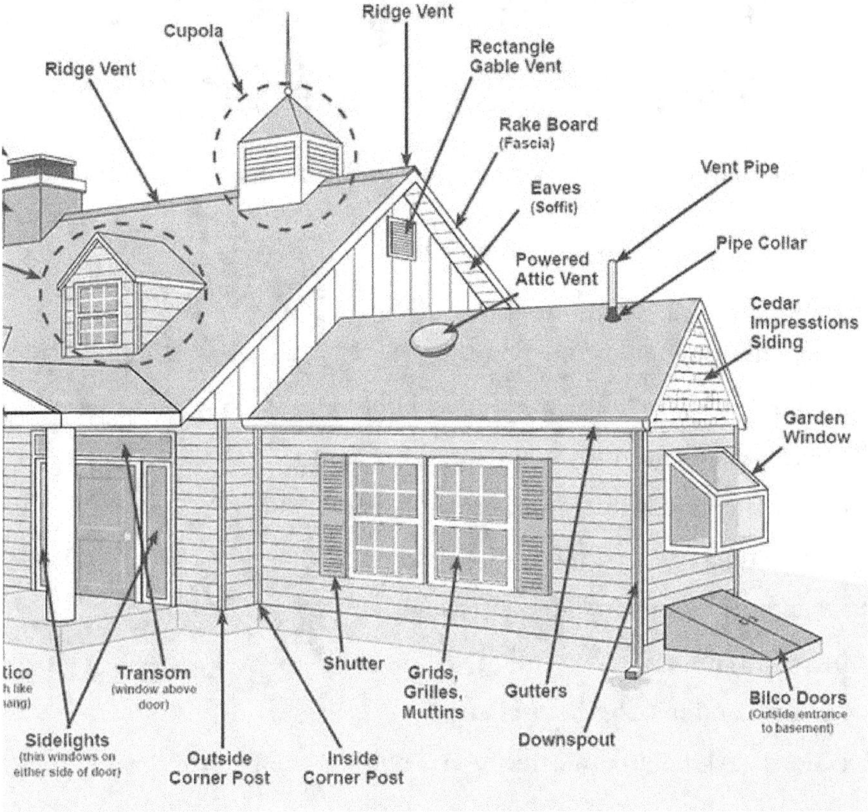

Porch Anatomy

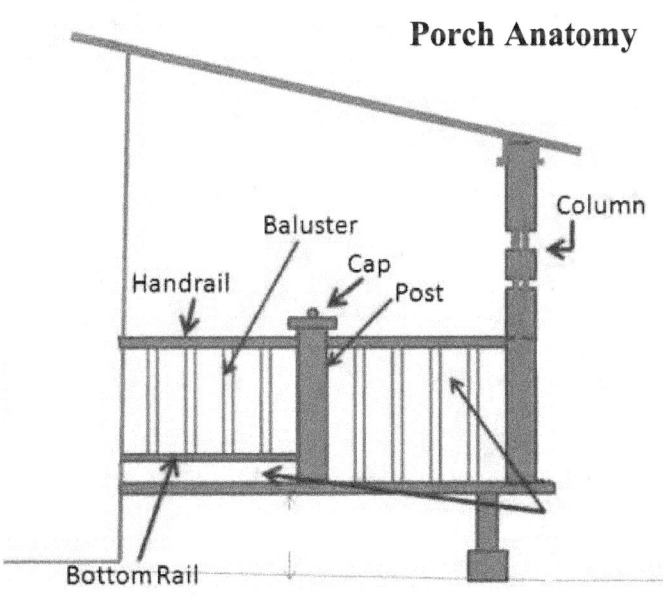

Are you struggling with getting jobs and making great money?

Looking back, over 15 years now, when I started out on my own, I wished he would have a painting mentor or a painting business coach to answer questions about the business side of things. I'm sure, if I had someone to consult with occasionally, they would have saved me from spending thousands of dollars in bad marketing choices, buying useless painting equipment and making poor client decisions. So, here I am offering my one-on-one painting business coaching services to you through –

https://www.paintingbizcoach.com

MY MONTHLY COACHING PROGRAM

- One weekly phone chat for 30 minutes.
- A weekly review of your business goals, issues and plans for the next week.
- Unlimited support, text support & email support for paint business marketing, sales and management.
- Month to month payments
- Receive my monthly newsletter.

Visit my website and subscribe today.

WATCH JEFF LOCKWOOD ON

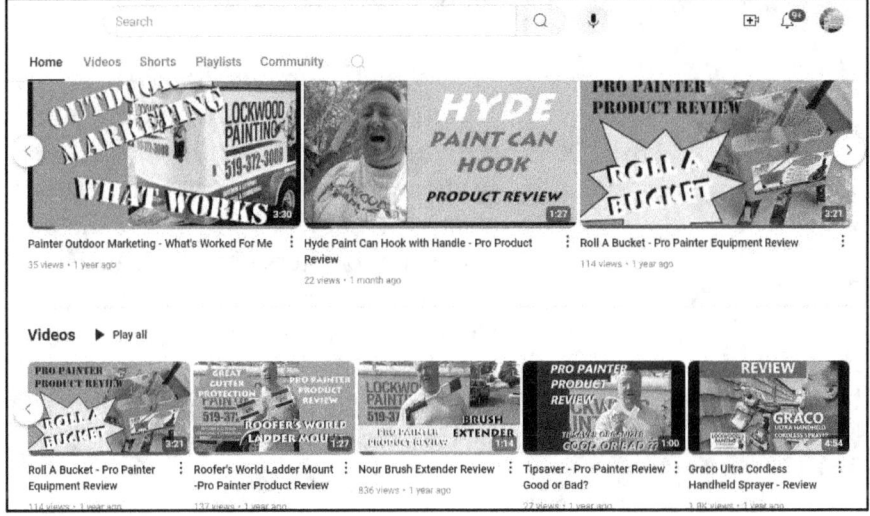

Painting Business Tips, Painter Product Reviews, Q&A Videos and More.

Check them out at -

https://www.youtube.com/@lockwoodpainting

Other Books by Jeff Lockwood, available on Amazon

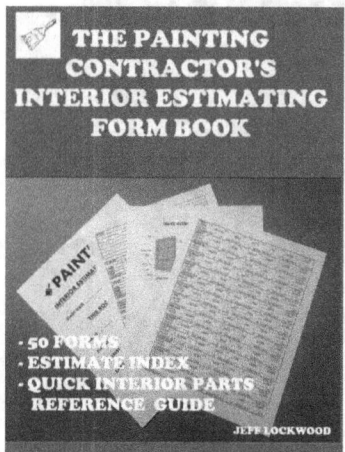

"The Painting Contractor's Interior Estimating Form Book" is a must-have tool for new painting contractors, featuring 50 four-sheet estimate forms in an 8.5 x 11-inch size. Created by an experienced contractor, it helps residential painters gather organized, detailed information for interior painting estimates. This form book simplifies the process, making estimating for various interior painting and decorating projects more accurately and efficiently.

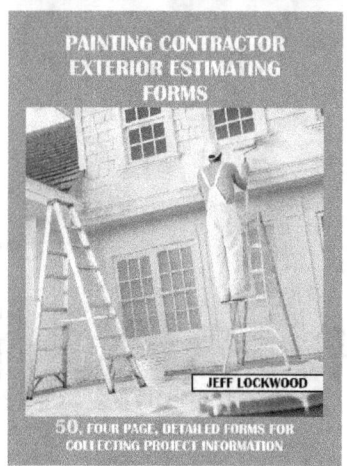

"Painting Contractor Exterior Estimating Forms" is a practical tool designed for new painting contractors. It features 50 four-sheet estimate forms in a convenient 8.5 x 11-inch size, helping residential painters gather organized details for exterior painting estimates. Created by an experienced contractor, it streamlines the estimating process, making it faster, easier, and more accurate for various exterior painting and staining projects.

"The Painting Contractor Estimate Request Call Log" is the perfect tool for residential painting contractors looking to stay organized and keep track of important business calls related to their projects. With dedicated sections for recording date, time, client name, phone number, project details, you'll have all the information you need to manage your client's first communications efficiently

www.ingramcontent.com/pod-product-compliance
Lightning Source LLC
Chambersburg PA
CBHW071833210526
45479CB00001B/114